Also by RACHEL TOOR

Fiction

On the Road to Find Out

Nonfiction

Admissions Confidential: An Insider's Account
of the Elite College Selection Process

The Pig and I

Personal Record: A Love Affair with Running

MISUNDERSTOOD

Baby Iris. Was there ever a sweeter face?

Rachel Toor

MISUNDERSTOOD

Why the Humble Rat May Be Your Best Pet Ever

Farrar Straus Giroux
New York

Farrar Straus Giroux Books for Young Readers
175 Fifth Avenue, New York 10010

fiercereads.com

Library of Congress Control Number: 2016930725

Our books may be purchased in bulk for promotional, educational, or business use. Please
contact your local bookseller or the Macmillan Corporate and Premium Sales Department at
(800) 221-7945 ext. 5442 or by e-mail at MacmillanSpecialMarkets@macmillan.com.

For Pop,
and for my Hon-Fat

Contents

MISUNDERSTOOD

Introduction

For three and a half years I was in love with someone the size of a hot dog bun. Her name was Iris. She was a rat.

Iris would follow me around the house, gallop into the kitchen to stand by the fridge and twirl for broccoli, and snuggle with me in bed. She would come when I called her name, or "Poochiesnoggins," "Little I," "Ireechi," "Honeymunchkin," "Sweet Potato," or any of the seven thousand other terms of endearment I had for her.

The poochiesnoggins would ride on my shoulder to visit friends, spar with my fingers when I typed, pounce on pieces of string like a predator, leap for the unalloyed joy of having a physical body, and groom herself until every single hair—and I mean every single hair—was perfectly in place.

Never greedy, Iris would accept any piece of offered food, even if she wasn't hungry, in which case she'd stash it away for later, sometimes under the bed, sometimes in one of my shoes. She greeted strangers as if she were being paid to make them feel welcome.

Scooping her up like a flower, I'd hold her close to my face and inhale her scent. She smelled like perfume, something between cotton candy and lilacs. Sweet but never cloying, Iris was like a furry sachet.

She used her tiny four-fingered hands that looked like twinkling stars to hold fast on to things, me included.

In the years since Iris died—and I'm giving away the end of the story here: Iris died—she has continued to lodge in my heart.

Living with and loving Iris made me realize how many people just don't get rats. I thought about this. Talked about it. And looked for books that might help me understand the venomous hatred directed toward these poor rodents. I knew I wasn't the only one who appreciated these critters. Where was the book that paid tribute to the playfulness, warmth, dignity, and intelligence of rats, perhaps the world's most unfairly reviled species? I couldn't find it.

A standard piece of advice established authors give aspiring writers is to write the book you want to read. That's what you're holding in your hand. Honestly, I would have preferred someone else to do the hard work of writing. I'm pretty lazy. But I looked and looked and couldn't find any books that set out to extol the many (many, many) virtues of domesticated rats.

It took me a long time to finish this one. More than ten years. When I started it I did so with Iris on my lap. Sometimes she'd climb onto my shoulder. Sometimes she'd chase my fingers as they tapped away at the keyboard. I read parts of it aloud to her. She tended to sleep through those sessions, perking up only when she heard her name. Like most of us, Iris listened for the sound of her name.

When I had the chance to write about another passion of mine, running, I put aside my work on rats. Then I got busy and realized that years had gone by and my rat book still hadn't gotten done. (Note that use of the passive voice: *It hadn't gotten done.* Not *I hadn't done it.* That's a writer's way of letting herself off the hook.)

Then, because I believed in this project, I got serious. My agent and I worked for a year to get a proposal into shape.

Well, sort of.

In truth, I worked for a bit, got stuck, and then a few

months later Elise, my patient and encouraging agent, would shoot me an email saying, "Just checking in! How's it going?" I'd feel guilty, do some more work, and then get stuck again. Lather, rinse, repeat.

Finally, we had a book proposal. Elise sent it to a number of publishers and to my astonishment we soon had an offer. And then while we waited to hear back from the others, I got one of those out-of-the-blue emails that can change your life. Or at least, mine.

Dear Rachel,

I've enjoyed reading your pieces in *Running Times* and in the midst of a recent running-book-reading jag, I've found your *Personal Record* to be a highlight. One of the things I like most about it is your gift for turning ordinary, easily overlooked things, such as your overstuffed drawers of running clothes or the pantry filled with energy bars and sports drinks, into material for your stories or springboards for your plots.

As a children's book editor as well as a runner, I was also interested to see your chapter about coaching the high-school XC team as well as to read in your bio about your experience dealing with (and writing for and about) college-age kids and the college experience.

All of which makes me wonder if you've ever considered writing fiction, in particular a YA novel about a high-school girl runner? I don't know what that story might be but I like the idea of a book with this subject. A book that tells a good tale and in the process gets at the heart of the magic of running for its adherents, and maybe convinces a few kids to lace up and hit the road.

Curious to hear from you if you are interested in discussing this.

Holy cow! This letter came from Wes Adams, a book editor at Farrar Straus Giroux, the publisher of my dreams. Of course I couldn't imagine writing a novel. I didn't write fiction, didn't know how to do that, but man oh man how flattering to be asked.

After running around the house screaming, scaring the bejesus out of my fifty-pound mutt, Helen, I wrote back an email filled with girly exclamation points and said, "YES! I would love to talk!"

As soon as I hit Send I realized this was silly. Who was I kidding? I couldn't write a novel. And I had finally gotten some traction on my rat book.

The editor and I talked and I blathered on about my self-doubt. I said, "I can't write a novel."

Wes said, "That's ridiculous."

Wait, what?

He encouraged me to try.

I tried.

I sent him pages that, the minute they left my out-box, I realized were horrible. Embarrassing. Painful.

Wes would read them and say, "Just keep going."

I'd say, "No, I already scrapped them and started again."

I could practically hear him put his head in his hands.

If Wes didn't get back to me in four hours, I'd decide he had come to his senses, realized that this was a lost cause, and given up. Turned out he had other projects, other authors, a family, you know, something besides me and my crappy attempt at a novel.

In the meantime, another editor, this one at a huge commercial publishing house, wanted to have a conversation with me about my rat book.

On a Friday afternoon I had a conference call with that editor, the marketing manager, and a publicist. The editor, young and enthusiastic, had some ideas about a different way to shape the manuscript. It was great to get her feedback.

I knew the marketing and publicity people wanted to suss out what I'd be like in terms of promoting the book. I was thrilled to discover the publicist was superexcited about the project.

"We could make rats the new 'it' pet!" he said.

That would be . . . good? The conversation seemed to be going well. The publicist, clearly an animal person, wanted to know where he could get a rat. I gave him some suggestions.

Then he wanted to know about my rat situation.

I explained, as I had written in the proposal, that Iris had died and I now had a rodent killer of a dog.

"Well, could you get a rat when the book comes out?"

Patiently—at least I tried to be patient—I explained again about Helen, and how she'd already taken out three squirrels and nine marmots and I couldn't sleep in the same bed with her if she became a rat assassin. It was hard enough to forgive her for her outdoor trespasses.

"Well," he said, "could you borrow a rat when the book comes out?"

Good grief.

It all became clear to me. The publicity guy wanted to send me on the circuit as a crazy rat lady. I imagined him booking me on talk shows. I'd sit there with a rent-a-rat on my shoulder and the host would make a face, extend his hands in mock fear, and say, "Plague!"

I'd try to engage in a serious conversation and explain

how smart and sweet and funny rats are. The host would start in on the tail.

I'd struggle not to get, you know, rattled and he'd make some pun about being rat-tled.

When I hung up from the conference call I was, indeed, rattled.

Over the weekend I thought about what it would take to get me to write that book and endure the kind of publicity stunts the company might require of me. The publisher didn't do small, quirky books. They wanted big bestsellers. I am, as you may have already gathered, an author of small, quirky books.

Quick as you can say "No rent-a-rats!" I realized I didn't want to write the book they wanted to publish.

And working with Wes on the novel was turning out to be a blast.

But I had spent so many years on the rat project. I had tracked down academic research, talked to scientists and rat lovers, bought tons of books about diseases for the few interesting facts I could glean about the poor critters who sometimes carried them. I'd gotten two research grants from my university for this long-term project on rats. Could I forget about all of that and focus on the novel?

I sure could.

~~~~

At that point I had published three books of nonfiction. My first, *Admissions Confidential* (I wanted to call it *Admissions Impossible*), was an account of my time as an admissions officer at Duke, a book I wrote because when I left that job I felt dirty and I wanted people to understand how the application process worked, and didn't work.

Wes wanted a novel that would make those who didn't get what motivated us nutty runners want to give running a whirl. I was down with that, but I also wanted to atone for my admissions book, which I wrote because I thought it would be helpful for kids and parents to know that even if they did everything "right," they still probably wouldn't get into a fancy-pants school. That message depressed a lot of folks and now I wanted to say the rest of what I thought: It doesn't matter if you don't get what you think you want. The quality of your life does not depend on which sticker you put on the back of your car. There are zillions of ways to get an education, a good education.

In *On the Road to Find Out* I gave a pet rat named Walter to my main character, Alice, a girl despondent about not getting into her first-choice school who decides on a whim to take up running. I figured that Alice could become a geeky little rat researcher, just like me, and share the cool rodent knowledge she (we) loved to unearth. The funnest part (yes, I sometimes use words like *funnest*) was writing the character of Walter, whom I based, of course, on my darling Iris.

When the novel came out I decided I would consider the novel and myself a success if I got emails from girls (and women) telling me any of the following things:

1. The book helped ease some of the worry about the college admissions process;

2. The book got them to start running;

3. The book made them want a pet rat.

I am here to tell you that by my own lights, I am a big fat success.

When I talked about *On the Road to Find Out* I often told the story of how Walter the rat came into the novel. A number of folks said I should go ahead and finish the rat book. No, I countered, I'm working on another novel.

But after enough people say the same thing to you, you start to listen. I brought up the idea with Wes and he asked to see the original book proposal. After reading it, he was unconvinced. It was too long and too academic sounding. It didn't grab him. Could I come up with something more fun—something that used all the amusing facts I'd learned about rats and let the world get to know my beloved Poochie-snoggins?

I sure could. That sounded like a book I wanted to read. And to write.

In *Misunderstood*, I hope to take you with me on my journey to find answers to my rat questions, starting with: Why do so many people hate rats?

I will consider this book a success if I get emails from folks who say that I've described the way they feel about their beloved pets, and also from those who have come to understand how and why these sweet creatures make such good companions. I want to tell you about all the cool stuff I've learned (and spare you the boring junk). I want you to get as excited as I am about the world of rats and the people who love them.

And no, I still don't have another rat. Now, when I need a rodent fix, I visit my godrats, Fern and Laurel, whose adorableness you can see throughout this book.

When *Misunderstood* comes out and I'm forced to do the inevitable public appearances, I hope that people will show up at my talks and readings with vermin on their shoulders; in my fantasy world I imagine speaking to huge roomfuls of rats and their people. Their people are, of course, my people: a diverse, fun, and fascinating group, as you will see if you keep reading.

Kara Loyd's "Ratvocates" are tiny lobbyists for rat equality

The Haters Gonna Hate, Hate, Hate, Hate, Hate

Why do so many people abhor/fear/detest rats?

Iris was my second rat.

My first, Hester, I got after college when I lived in New York City and worked in publishing. Hester and I had a rocky start. She had been raised in a laboratory and had never been handled. Early in our relationship she bit me. Twice. Not hard, not enough to draw blood, but as a signal that I needed to slow down and let her adjust to a new world order of no longer living in a lab. Her affectionate nature outweighed her fear, and we soon came to love each other.

Hester was the perfect apartment-mate. She never cared if I stayed out late, as long as I let her leave her cage for playtime when I got home. She didn't need to go for walks, though I sometimes took her, perched on my shoulder, for strolls around Gramercy Park. When I lived with Hester I learned how misunderstood rats were by the general public—even people who claimed to love animals seemed to feel no compunction about saying "ick" or "gross" when it came to rats, and not just the strangers who saw us on our infrequent rambles. My friends, all of whom knew how much I adored Hester, sometimes made mean remarks about my roomie.

When I met my future ex-husband he realized that the way to my heart was through my rat. He let her play on him, saved tasty morsels of food for her, and when she got sick at the fairly old age of three, he drove us to the vet and held me while I cried. For a long time, I couldn't drive past Hester Street in lower Manhattan without turning into a sniveling wreck.

My future ex-husband convinced me to move in with him by promising we could get a dog. We did. My wonderful mutt Hannah lasted much longer than our marriage.

Then, when Iris came into my life, I remembered how rats are basically like tiny dogs but easier to live with in many ways. Iris, so laid back, so accepting, so willing to go with the flow, became more than a pet. She was a role model.

Having a rat made me think about lots of things, not the

least being why, when rats are clearly superior companions, so many people are disgusted by them.

Try to imagine describing a friend and having people respond, *Eeeew! Redheads are soooooo gross!* Or, *People who talk with a Southern accent creep me out.* Or, *I hate tall people.* (I do, actually, hate tall people. Well, not *hate* them, but a jealousy this strong can feel like hatred. In fact, some of my best friends are tall.)

Most of us have learned it's not okay to smush a diverse group of people into an easily reduced and quickly dismissed lump. Most of us know that even in a field of daisies that look identical, small differences make each one unique if we bother to look closely enough.

When I hear smart, educated, socially aware folks say something as dumb as "I hate rats," I unfriend them.

No I don't.

Though I'd like to.

Instead I remember how bigotry and prejudice rely on ignorance to thrive. And then I try to teach them.

"If you don't like rats," I say in the gentlest, most teacherly tone I can muster, "perhaps it's because you haven't gotten to know one. Have you ever met a rat?"

Then I steel myself like a football player on the line waiting for the hike. I know what's coming. I brace myself.

I wait. It usually doesn't take more than a few seconds.

And there it is: "The tail!" they wail. "I just can't take the tail!"

Even the most articulate of my friends can't find the words to describe what they don't like about a rat's tail. So let's talk about the tail.

It's long. Yep. It's long. That's because rats use their tails for balance. They can climb ropes, maintain equipoise in precarious positions, stand on their back feet, and use their tails like the poles circus performers carry on the high wire.

It's naked, or at least that's what some people who have never examined one up close think. Why would a naked tail be so upsetting? Perhaps when we see animals missing patches of hair we believe they're sick. Maybe that's it. People think a hairless tail is less healthy than the bushy appendage found on, say, dog-taunting, birdseed-stealing, car-crash-causing squirrels.

Or maybe the naked tail reminds them of a snake. It's reasonable to be afraid of snakes, especially if you don't know which are the dangerous ones whose bites could kill you. But far from being naked and snaky, rats' tails are actually covered with tiny hairs and they do another important job. Rats can't pant like dogs, and they don't sweat like horses. They use their tails for thermoregulation. When they get too hot, the blood vessels in their tails swell in a process called vasodilation and the hot blood loses heat through the surface, and when it returns to the furry little body, it's cooled off. When a rat is cold, the vessels in the tail constrict and keep the blood—and therefore the rat—warmer. Pretty nifty trick, huh?

Once I parry the thrusts against the tail, I expect the haters to continue with another line of attack, and I know what's coming.

Rats are dirty. Filthy. They spread disease. And then, gaining momentum, finding their footing by searching what they remember from high-school history, the haters get to where I know they're headed: *Plague! They caused plague!*

I take a deep breath. I force the corners of my mouth to tilt up. I don't want to be that girl who blames someone for not knowing any better, for being, well, unenlightened. Making myself small and unthreatening, hunching, moderating my voice from the shrill tone that wants to escape, I say, "Well, not exactly."

Rats are not dirty. If you see a dirty rat, he's probably sick. They live in grungy places because humans are sloppy and wasteful and throw away all sorts of great and useful stuff. Rats profit from our profligate ways. They settle in populous areas like cities where lots of people leave lots of garbage. In places where there are fewer humans and less garbage, like the vast landscape of the American West, you don't find many rats.

Rats themselves are more fastidious about keeping clean than a heart surgeon afraid of being sued for malpractice.

They spread disease. Rats do spread disease. It's true. Hantavirus, eosinophilic meningitis, leptospirosis, rat-bite fever, Seoul virus, murine typhus, trichinosis—sure. But dogs, cats, cows, pigs, bunnies, birds, squirrels, and lots of other animals also carry these diseases, and more. Nature is filled with icky things. We've come to think that what's natural is good. But nature can kill you. If you need to be reminded of this, go for a walk outside during a big storm—rain, snow, thunder. Or stay inside during an earthquake. Or even just go for a swim in the ocean. There's some crazy scary stuff in the ocean and you'll never catch me anywhere near it.

As for plague, also scary. During the Middle Ages, when the Black Death took hold, it wiped out about a third of the population of Europe.

But rats did not cause plague. They, like humans, were casualties of it. Fleas carried the disease—in the form of the bacterial microbe *Yersinia pesits*—and they infected the rats they lived on, who itched, scratched, and then died.

It's not the meek who shall inherit the earth, it's the insects. Fleas found their way from the bodies of the rats they killed to humans, who died and were too ignorant to blame the correct critter.

Fleas spread plague, people! Not rats.

If you want to know more about this, you can find a plague of books written on plague. The malady existed well before the Black Death—people afflicted with plague-like symptoms appear in the Bible, in Periclean Athens, in the ancient Fertile Crescent, in early-fourteenth-century China. And it still exists on a large number of plague-infected but adorable prairie dogs in the western United States. Where there are very few rats.

New evidence links the spread of plague to—are you ready?—gerbils. I can't tell you how this delights me. I have a suspicion that the "pocket pets"—gerbils, hamsters, guinea pigs, ferrets, hedgehogs—got together and hired a public relations firm to convince people that they make better companions than rats. Hamsters are vicious, guinea pigs are spastic, gerbils are anxious, ferrets are stinky, and hedgehogs can turn themselves into medieval torture weapons. Gerbils spread plague? Hooray! I can't wait to see those jittery little creeps go down. (Not that there's anything wrong with gerbils. They just can't hold a candle to the brightness of my favorite rodents.)

They destroy things. The most knowledgeable of the rat haters may mention destruction caused by rats. It's undeniable: Wild rats cost humans zillions of dollars. They eat tons of grain and chew through wires, sometimes causing outages and fires. They even gnaw on concrete. Wild rats do this because they are trying to survive, just like other pests: insects, wolves, hawks, deer. But how often does someone claim to hate Bambi?

It's understandable not to like the things that scare us. Wild rats tend to come out at twilight. We don't like things that go bump in the night, or that skitter and scratch. We don't like knowing they're there and that we can't fully see them. Rats are good at staying out of our way, and at most we catch only a glance of a wild one. A tail. A dark shape scurrying in the periphery of our vision.

Rats are excellent at procreation. A single pair of rats and their offspring may produce fifteen thousand descendants in a year. Exterminators are often the biggest admirers of the success of rats. They point out that when rats are killed off, the pregnancy rate of the surviving rats increases and the survivors are hardier. They gain weight rapidly and become stronger.

I think that's amazing and impressive.

~ ~ ~ ~

When I talk to haters about their problems with rats, I can relate to their fears of the wild ones. I would no more bring a coyote into my home than I would a wild rat.

"But," I say, "I'm not talking about wild rats. I'm talking about domestic rats, love bugs like my little Iris."

"Same thing," they say.

"Ick," they say.

"No, no, no," I say. "You just don't understand."

Iris belonged to the species *Rattus norvegicus*, also known as the brown rat, common rat, street rat, sewer rat, Hanover rat, Norway rat, brown Norway rat, Norwegian rat, or wharf rat. Iris was not brown, did not live on streets or in sewers, and her forebears came from neither Hanover nor Norway. In fact, the critters called Norway rats are about as Scandinavian as I am. Which is to say, not at all. Iris and her kind came originally from Asia, probably China. Norway is the wrong home, people. Just another misunderstanding.

After too many of these conversations, I started wondering, Is rat hating a worldwide thing? Is it a part of being human?

Um, not really.

People in other countries have profound respect for these resourceful creatures. In the Chinese zodiac, the rat is the first animal of the year. As with many origin stories, it's not clear exactly why this is. Most of the accounts have it that someone, either the Buddha or the Jade Emperor, called on the animals to race. According to one story, the rat came in first because he got up earliest. Some say because rats have four digits on their front paws and five on their back, that makes them special and they get to be in first place.

But another story holds that when the cat and the rat, the worst swimmers, figured out they had to cross a river, they asked the good-natured ox if they could have a ride on his back. Midway across the rat pushed the cat into the water. When they neared the shore, the clever rat jumped ahead and beat the ox. So the rat is first, the ox second, and the poor cat didn't even make it into the zodiac.

Those born in the Year of the Rat are said to be ambitious, smart, quick-witted, resourceful, curious, shrewd, hardworking, careful, artistic, talky, charming, energetic, sociable, and observant. (On the not-so-good side, they may also be greedy, jealous, suspicious, selfish, critical, arrogant, amoral, edgy, and agitated.)

In Hindu mythology, Lord Ganesh, the remover of obstacles, rides a rat. Ganesh is a cool dude: he's the god of beginnings, of letters and learning, arts and culture, intellect and wisdom. It's easy to pick him out in the pantheon of

Hindu deities: he has the head of an elephant with one tusk and a trunk, a beer belly, and an indeterminate number of arms, but always more than two.

In northwest India, the temple of Karni Mata is devoted to the worship of the rat goddess, and people come from all over the world to the small town of Deshnoke to see the twenty thousand rats who are fed milk and grain by priests. It's considered an honor to eat food that has been sampled by a rat. I totally get this: each time I shared a meal or treat with Iris, I felt blessed.

So, right, not everyone in the world hates rats. But do you know who does? New Yorkers. New Yorkers hate rats. They scorn and condemn the rodents who live in close proximity to them. Even the most tolerant of animal lovers will quail at the sight of a scampering, scurrying subway rat; people who escort spiders outside or shoo flies away will often take pleasure in exterminating a varmint. This is too bad, because for people living in apartments who don't have the time or ability to take a dog for regular walks, a rat can be the perfect pet.

If you love New York and you hate rats, I have a book recommendation for you: Robert Sullivan's 2004 bestseller *Rats: Observations on the History and Habitat of the City's Most Unwanted Inhabitants.*

For a while after I'd read his book, I thought of Robert Sullivan as the enemy. The bad guy. The über-hater. He isn't, of course. He is more like my inspiration, my model, and my counterpoint. He's the reason I wanted to write this book. I'm trying here to provide the flip side of what he did.

In so many ways, *Rats* is wonderful. Sullivan is a collector of weird information and has the agility of an Olympic gymnast (or a rat) at jumping between topics and linking disparate ideas. *Rats* is a book about New York City as much as anything. He recounts the landlord-tenant wars of the 1960s; the sanitation strike of 1968; the geography of Wall Street. It's a book rich in information.

He gives us the basic history: most city rats are *Rattus norvegicus*, the brown rat, that Asian critter mistakenly thought to be originally from Norway. *Rattus rattus*, the black rat, got pushed out by its bigger brown cousin, though it still lives in some coastal southern cities and, he says, Los Angeles. Hollywood is apparently full of rats.

Montana was the last state in America to be settled by *Rattus norvegicus*. Sullivan tells us: "Several yearly rat settlements in Montana failed or were wiped out with poisons and traps, but the brown rat finally colonized Lewistown in 1920, and in 1938 the dump in Missoula became the site of an escaped colony of laboratory rats, domesticated *Rattus norvegicus*."

In fact, I got Iris when I lived in Missoula. Often my running buddies and I would do the "dump run," where we trotted from downtown, through the dump, and over Waterworks Hill. We frequently encountered mule deer, with their big ears, white tails, and funny, bouncing gait, and white-tailed deer, who looked much the same as mule deer to me. Once, I saw a coyote, and occasionally a bald eagle would soar overhead. But I never saw rats.

Not surprising, according to Sullivan. Rats learned to go where there are people, and there just aren't that many folks living in the big rectangular states on the left side of the map.

In Billings, Montana, it is illegal to keep pet rats. It is also illegal for married women to go fishing alone on Sundays, and for unmarried women to fish alone at all. But if you ride your horse to school, the state must provide food and shelter for him or her while you are being educated. It's the law. That's Montana for you.

To the north, Alberta, Canada, boasts about its status as "an essentially rat-free province." If you're found aiding and abetting a rat (or a neighbor who keeps rats), you could be fined up to five thousand dollars.

Sullivan's book is an unusual and wonderful bit of nature writing set in an urban environment. He describes his excursions with exterminators as if they were out hunting grizzly bears. Sullivan doesn't actually come face-to-face with a rat until nearly the end of the book, when, with Dan and Anne from the New York City health department, he manages to trap some rats in order to anesthetize them with halothane, take blood from their hearts, and then kill—or try to kill—them. The author and Dan are impressed by the toughness of the rats.

The only person in the book who ever says anything nice about rats is Anne. Sullivan quotes her as saying things like "I think rats are so underappreciated" and "Rats are the smartest creatures." And, when looking at a trapped rat, "Look at this rat. This rat is beautiful." Hard not to love Anne. No one else the author meets ever sees the rats as anything other than disgusting.

Sullivan writes,

> Both pet rats and laboratory rats are *Rattus norvegicus*, but they are not wild and therefore, I would emphasize, are not the subject of this book. Sometimes pet rats are called fancy rats. But if anyone has picked up this book to learn about fancy rats, then they should put this book down right away; none of the rats mentioned herein are at all fancy.

Got that? *Rats* is a book for the haters. Though anyone interested in rats would in fact like Sullivan's book because it's freaking awesome. In an afterword to the paperback edition, Sullivan writes about his experiences on book tours and responds in print to the questions people most frequently ask him.

He says,

> Let me make this next answer perfectly clear: I think rats are really, really gross, though through no fault of their own. I think it is our fault, actually. We humans are always looking for a species to despise, especially since we can and do act despicably ourselves.

He also feels compelled to clarify something he thought he had addressed in the book (he had) but still got called out on: his interest is in wild rats. "People often brought pictures of their pet rats to share with me," he writes. "At one reading in Berkeley, California, I thought I was going to have a rat riot on my hands when a small group of people showed up thinking I was against pet rats or something—and again, I'm not, I swear. It's just that wild rats aren't at all like pet rats."

In a footnote he explains that the fancy rat came about as a result of Jack Black, who caught rats for Queen Victoria and also sold some to the ladies of the time who fancied rats, women like Beatrix Potter, author of *Peter Rabbit*.

Sullivan is such a skilled writer you're happy to read about the strength of a rat's teeth—harder, he says, than aluminum, lead, copper, or iron. Superman teeth is what they are, with the strength of steel. And he lays to rest the idea that rats gnaw to grind down their front teeth, which grow at a rate of five inches per year. He says they wear down naturally.

So lots of great, gross stuff in this book. Lots of ammunition for those who want to squeal and squawk. Plenty of information, both trivial and profound, for the haters who are gonna hate, hate, hate, hate, hate.

No one ever hated Iris. Not one person who met that darling honeymunchkin failed to be charmed. All you had to do was spend some time with her.

When she got bored and felt puppyish, she'd start messing with my fingers or the pages of my book to get attention. I always stopped what I was doing to play.

We often played Whack-a-Rat, where she would disappear into the folds of a blanket and then pop her head out. I'd tap her on the head and she'd retreat, only to come charging back a few seconds later.

I never taught her to come when called. I just said her name, sometimes I clapped my hands, and she would bound over to me like a superhero.

When I had people visit, she'd climb on their shoes. She'd

haul herself onto their laps. She'd grab their fingers and give them a gentle manicure.

When I sat at my computer she liked to park herself on my lap and sleep. Sometimes she'd leap up and patrol the desk, nosing papers out of the way, sampling a bit of pencil. She loved to chase my fingers as they flew across the keys. As charming as this was, I discouraged the behavior. Not because I minded when she added interestingly spelled words to my prose but because I feared she'd get one of her tiny digits squeezed.

When I lay in bed at night, reading or watching TV, Iris cuddled with me. Or she raced around the bed, often peering over the side. Rarely did she venture far in her explorations. When she did, she'd come charging back as soon as I called her name.

Iris was as much like the rats Sullivan hunted in New York City as you are like an Indian deity with the head of an elephant and a bunch of extra arms.

If you want to read a book about how disgusting wild rats are, pick up Robert Sullivan's *Rats*. If you want to know how and why a domesticated rat might be the pet of your dreams, stick with me.

Iris and her babysitter Sage in 2006

Who You Calling Cute?

What makes us think something or someone is cute?

When he first met Iris, my friend Jason expressed real surprise. "But she's so cute," he gushed. "I wasn't expecting her to be cute."

Jason is a smart guy. He had managed to insult me and compliment Iris in one sentence. Why didn't he think she'd be cute, and what made him change his mind? I'm sure her personality had something to do with it. She made everyone feel special just by paying attention to them: *Hello! Do you want to hold me? Can I climb on you? I like you! Let's be friends!*

My hunch is that Jason's reaction had something to do with

Iris's coloring. When people who don't know any better think of rats, they picture wild skitterers the color of sewers.

Another friend, Dan, a horse guy, said when he saw a photo of Iris, "You didn't tell me your rat was a paint." Iris's coat, like Dan's gelding's, was a combination of white and colored splotches. He too admitted she was cute.

Of course both of them knew that if they wanted to remain friends with me they couldn't say anything bad about Iris.

But what, I began to wonder, makes something cute? Why are hamsters considered cute and rats aren't? What does *cute* even mean?

In the 1700s, the word was a shortened version of *acute*, meaning sharp or quick-witted, clever or shrewd. Would anyone use it that way today?

Nope.

I'm going to tell you right now, I hate cute.

Cute is all earnestness and exaggerated simplicity.

Cute has no sharp edges.

Cute indulges the awkward, the ungainly, the stupid, the round, the slow, the lumbering, the static, the wide.

Cute is the opposite of threatening; one of the things most likely to make something seem cute is vulnerability. We want to pick it up and protect it.

Cute is submissive, paws in the air, throat exposed.

Cute sits upright with a big furry head and huge open eyes, paws resting on a rotund belly.

Cute has long eyelashes and a soft, curvy body.

Cute cries in ways that make you laugh.

I'm no different from anyone in that if I see a puppy, or a foal, or a baby of any animal other than a human, I lose my words and can utter only long, high, vowel sighs—*Ooooh! Eeee! Awww!*

On the other hand, the sight of dolls with faces like vegetables makes me want to barf. Big pink bows, I ♥ U notes, sweaters with cats, emojis—fine for you; not for me.

As a kid, I struggled around smart girls who did well in school, had creative impulses, and yet giggled after every sentence they uttered. I always felt like I wasn't getting the joke. What was so funny?

No doubt my approach to the world was overly serious and perhaps a tad harsh. But inappropriate giggling seemed to diminish these friends of mine, to render them less impressive. Early on I had a feminist sensibility and bridled whenever women—girls—sought to undercut their strength. I viewed giggling, "up talking" (ending every sentence as if it's a question), and displays of cuteness as a way to say *Don't worry about me—I'm no threat. I'm just happy, silly, giggly, soft, cuddly. Don't fret—I won't beat you in a race or get a higher score on a math test than you, big boy. I won't outearn you or make you feel small by pointing out all the ways in which you're stupid and wrong. Look! I'm harmless!*

Now when I meet girls who giggle when they speak, I understand they're trying to fit in. Most kids grow up being told by their parents they are beautiful and unique snow-flakes, which is very nice and all but not so comforting when what these teens want most is to be like everyone else. Appearing nonthreatening is a way to get along.

The problem with cute is that it can shut down thought. In one of my favorite essays, "Politics and the English Lan-guage," George Orwell makes a case against using clichés because, he says, they "think your thoughts for you." Cute demands that you stop thinking and just feel all warm and fuzzy. Laziness in imbibing social values can deaden us and keep us from challenging the status quo.

Given how crabby I am about babies and rainbows and lollipops, imagine my horror at having to spend time at ground zero of cute, what I call "The Unhappiest Place on Earth": Disney World. I used to have to go there to lead marathon pace groups and it was sheer torture. The place, not the pacing.

I know, I know, some people love all things Disney. You

may be one of them. I'm sorry. I shouldn't complain. But I do. I like very little about that industrial entertainment complex except for this: Walt Disney, the man who inflicted cute on us in ways our culture may never recover from, loved mice.

When Walt cast about for an animal to star as a cartoon character, he came up with Mortimer Mouse. His wife, Lillian, didn't balk at the species selection but found the name pretentious. Flash forward to a figure today recognizable by nothing more than three black circles. Three black circles that manage to embody cute.

It was an interesting choice. Why did Walt Disney think Mickey Mouse would be a compelling character?

As I went in search of the answer, I found a fascinating essay by the late evolutionary biologist Stephen Jay Gould.

When Gould was five years old his father took him to a place far better for kids than Disney World or Disneyland: the American Museum of Natural History, a place my grandfather took me nearly every time I visited New York City. There, instead of seeing princesses and costumed cartoon characters, a kid gets to marvel at the very real and very weird natural world. When Gould saw the skeleton of a *T. rex*, he decided to become a paleontologist. And he did. He also became one of those rare scientists who can write books and essays for nonspecialists—a bestselling author who happened to be a professor at Harvard.

In "A Biological Homage to Mickey Mouse," a widely anthologized 1979 essay that first appeared in *Natural History* magazine, Gould uses the occasion of Mickey's birthday to chart the physiological changes in the cartoon character. Mickey, instead of aging and growing up like the rest of us, has, over the course of his career, seemed to have found the fountain not just of youth but of age regression.

Over the years, Mickey's features became more juvenile. In the beginning, Mickey looked like a rat and acted like a creep. His first film, *Steamboat Willie*, in 1928, showed Mickey as a tweaker of a pig's nipples, a cranker of a goat's tail, a smasher, pounder, and banger of the other animals he encountered. (Minnie, I'm sorry to tell you, was no better.) Fan letters, and complaints from those who were not fans, caused the studio to draw Mickey into line. He became a kinder, gentler representative of what would become the Disney nation.

As Mickey got older, he turned benign and kind of boring. Gould makes a case that Mickey's transformation at the hands of Disney animators follows a "progressive juvenilization." In other words, Mickey went through the aging process in reverse. His head got bigger and more childlike, his nose got thicker and less pointy, his eyes went from plain black dots to having pupils. His ears moved back on his head, farther from his nose, giving him a rounded face rather than a sloping forehead. His former ratlike appearance vanished into the bland profile of a chubby little kid.

Sure, it makes sense to appease the fan base and rewrite Mickey's character to be more appealing. But why draw him to look so young? I mean, he interacted in the world as a grown-up and had an indeterminate relationship with Minnie; he was a manly mouse. Why make him look like a baby?

Gould looks to the work of Konrad Lorenz, the father of ethology, the study of animal behavior, to answer this question. He cites one of Lorenz's most famous articles to help him figure out what's going on with Mickey. Gould reports Lorenz believed baby features—"a relatively large head, predominance of the brain capsule, large and low-lying eyes, bulging cheek region, short and thick extremities, a springy elastic consistency, and clumsy movements"—triggered an "innate releasing mechanism" for adult care. In other words, we see those small blobby things and it makes us go *aww* and *oochie-coochie*. Gould points out that there is much debate about whether the response is innate and inherited, or learned, but decides not to enter it. He does agree, however, with the notion that round is cute.

He shows how Lorenz generalized his ideas to fit with our responses to animals: "We are, in short," Gould writes, "fooled by an evolved response to our own babies, and we transfer our reaction to the same set of features in other animals." The argument goes that we prefer animals that look most like very young humans. "We are drawn to them, we cultivate them as pets, we stop and admire them in the wild—while we reject their small-eyed, long-snouted relatives who might make more affectionate companions or objects of admiration."

Aha! This explains the wrongheaded pet-store preference for charismatic mini pets, your eat-their-own-offspring hamsters; your darting, squeaking guinea pigs; your poop-all-over-the-place bunnies. These "pocket pets" look like babies, even when they're fully grown.

Rats get short shrift. And perhaps that's because they are pointy, not round. When we see pointy, we think wild. Domestication looks round. And round is cute. And cute is nonthreatening. Hello, Kitty!

Gould, an evolutionary biologist, spent his career in the shadow of Charles Darwin, thinking about and refining the great man's theory of evolution.

You will have heard, no doubt, of Charles Darwin. He starts his famous book, *On the Origin of Species*, by pointing out something that might seem obvious now: how much greater variety there is among domesticated animals (and plants) than there is in corresponding wild species. He notices that domestic ducks' wings weigh less and their legs weigh more than their wild relatives', possibly because they fly less and walk more; that the udders of cows and goats develop differently in countries where those animals are milked; and that domestic critters have droopy ears, possibly because they don't have to listen as carefully for danger.

Strange things happen to animals after they've lived with humans for generations. Their bodies change in both form and function. Multicolored dark coats that allow them to blend into their environments—which helped them in the wild—start to get patches of white. Their fur becomes wavy or curly. Snouts get shorter and wider. In some cases tails shrink down to stubs. Ears turn floppy. Think about the zillions of different breeds of dogs you've seen and how much variety there is. Weiner dogs look nothing like shar-peis who look nothing like French bulldogs. Now think about canines in the wilderness: wolves, coyotes, jackals. They all appear pretty similar. That's what wild looks like. Wild does not look like a pug.

Rats in subways and sewers appear, well, wild. Domesticated rats, on the other hand, come in a buffet of exquisite colors. They can have coats like paint horses or Siamese cats. They can be champagne-colored, or gray, or even blue like Remy in *Ratatouille*. You would no more mistake a pet rat for a sewer dweller than you would a parrot for a pigeon.

With domestication, behavior also changes. Where wild animals seem grown-up and aloof, snooty even, domesticated beasts act like needy babies—whining when they want something, barking for attention. You can't pull nonsense like that when you're out in the wilderness with others who might eat you.

There's a cool experiment about domestication I want to share with you. In 1959, Dmitri K. Belyaev, a Soviet geneticist who did not accept the Communist Party's scientific line and was forcibly "moved" to Siberia, became director of the Institute of Cytology and Genetics in Novosibirsk. (I don't know how to pronounce that either.) He set up an experiment with silver foxes to test the genetics of domestication. He selected the tamest foxes—those least fearful of human contact—and bred them with other tame-acting foxes. He did the same with the most aggressive ones.

After eight generations, the tame foxes began to tolerate human contact. The behavior of the two strains, tame and aggressive, each became more pronounced. Then Belyaev died, but his former graduate student Lyudmila N. Trut continued with his work. She published an article in *Scientific American* in 1999 that let the rest of the world know what the Siberian scientists had been up to. Big news. They had identified body-type and behavioral changes that occur with selection for tameness. Can you guess what they were? Think about what "wild" looks like. Now imagine going to the dog park and looking at who's playing. Right! Dogs, when compared to wolves, look more like puppies.

The tame Siberian foxes, like domesticated critters, started to have spotted rather than solid coats; patches of white showed up in their fur. Their heads became broader and their ears drooped.

Belyaev, I should mention, had realized it might be easier to experiment with a species that produces generations at a fast rate. He turned, naturally, to rats, and Trut carried on his work. In 2005, the reporter Nicholas Wade wrote in the *New York Times,* "When a visitor enters the room where the tame rats are kept, they poke their snouts through the bars to be petted. The other colony of rats has been bred from exactly the same stock, but for aggressiveness instead. These animals are ferocious." He quotes an animal behavior expert named Tecumseh Fitch as saying: "Imagine the most evil supervillain and the nicest, sweetest cartoon animal, and that's what these two strains of rat are like."

You can tame a wild animal, but that's different from

domestication, a process that takes place over many generations and involves selection for particular traits linked to the specific expression of genes.

Charles Darwin himself had figured all of this out. He noticed the floppier ears, the patches of white, the smaller jaws, but he didn't have the molecular biology to back up a theory of inheritance. He did note that certain traits went together: he claimed blue-eyed cats tended to be deaf.

Now that we know so much about genetics, scientists have figured out how these changes occur. When humans started living with animals and then breeding them, they selected those not inclined to fight or flee, animals who were less fearful. These traits linked to genes that also called for depigmentation (white spots) and—it pains me to say this—smaller forebrains. So when domesticated animals became friendlier, they may also have lost a bit of their smarts.

When the Siberian scientist Lyudmila Trut continued the work done by her mentor, Belyaev, she found that after fifteen years and more than thirty generations of rats, their fur became increasingly white. More than 70 percent of the rats had white bellies. Depigmentation goes along with domestication.

Learning this provoked in me another Aha! moment. When it comes to dogs, I prefer those whose ears stand up.

I have always believed they're smarter, though I never had any proof of this except for anecdotal evidence based on my own experience and prejudice. I'll take a supersmart wild-looking mutt over a slobberingly happy but dumb, droopy-eared Lab any day. Not that there's anything wrong with Labs.

Iris, a homey and domesticated rat, was mostly white except for her head and shoulders and some big splotches on her back. I always had a hard time explaining the color of her spots. I called them "fawn," because they looked like the coat of a baby deer. A light mixture of brown, honey, tan, and gray. I never knew how to describe her coat other than to say it was luminescent and rich.

Now I know the nonwhite parts of Iris were called "agouti," which is the color of wild rats. Agouti fur consists of hairs with bands of different colors.

Iris. Sweet, compliant, fearless Iris.

Cute? Yes, she sure was cute. But she also had just a touch of the wild.

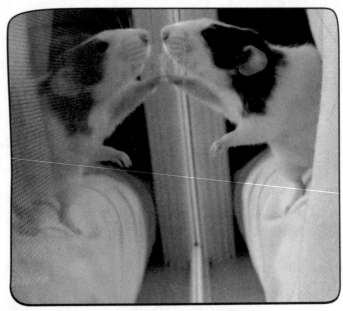

Laurel checking out her own image

In Search of Positive Images
Are there any good representations of rats?

I often thought I should have a bracelet made that read "WWID? What Would Iris Do?" That rat was a role model for me, and could be one for you, too.

Iris was:

Fastidiously clean (except for occasional tail-hygiene issues)

Always in a good mood

Welcoming to strangers

Eager to explore

Considerate of friends

Willing to share

Empathetic

Industrious

Athletic

Fearless

Funny

Gorgeous

A good sleeper

A thoughtful eater

Not a biter

Able to endure pain without complaint

Tender to dogs

Benevolent to children

I made this list of Iris's attributes years ago. It sounded to me like the description of a superhero, or of a celebrity I'd love to meet. Why then, I wondered, did I have to search so hard to find positive representations of rats in books, movies, and art?

When I saw *Ratatouille* I jumped for joy. Finally someone got it! If you haven't seen that movie, stop reading now and go get your hands on it. Do not go to school or work. Do not eat or sleep until you've watched it. You'll thank me.

Despite the snarky things I've said about Disney, this Oscar-winning film was a co-production between that producer of too much cuteness and Pixar; I bet old Walt would have loved it. The filmmakers studied how rats move and got it exactly right. Those animated characters embody the essence of ratness. Plus, the movie sends a message you can't argue with: everyone can do it (*it* being pretty much any art form), but not everyone will be great. And greatness can come from anywhere. It's a portrait of the artist as a young rat. If you get the DVD, you'll be treated to a short film called *Your Friend the Rat* in which the filmmakers, like me, try to get the haters' heads out of their butts.

So that's one.

What other movies star rats in positive roles?

Waiting.

Waiting.

Waiting.

Right.

It's hard to come up with any. Though you may by now have thought of a bunch of films where rats make an appearance, we're not interested in that kind of nasty business.

If we turn to other art forms, we're similarly shortchanged. Historically, most images of rats are of the wild variety and are about as far from warm and fuzzy as pictures of cockroaches.

Until recently, that is.

If you have access to a computer, you may have seen certain rat photographs that cause you to emit long vowel noises. Three women in particular have done much to showcase the charm and beauty of these amazing animals.

When you see Ellen Van Deelen's work, it's impossible not to squeal and coo. If you're reading this book now, chances are you squealed and cooed when you saw the cover. That's Moppy, one of Ellen's rats, holding a teddy bear. And on page 90, he's getting ready for a road trip.

Ellen lives in Holland. Her rat pictures have traveled the world and the World Wide Web. She has taken photos of rats playing miniature musical instruments, pushing grocery carts and baby carriages, sitting at tiny tables with tiny teacups and saucers, checking out a goldfish bowl, holding stuffed animals, and wearing sunglasses and straw hats.

It's hard not to wonder about the woman who created this amazing art. So I contacted her.

Did she always like rats? I asked.

Ellen replied, "I never liked rats! When I had to be in the pet shop, I even tried not to look at the cage where the rats were."

What happened?

"One day, I came, and saw in a cage a little dark brown animal curled up in a corner. I asked what it was, and the owner told me it was a rat. He was alone in the cage."

You see where this is going.

"The next week, I came again, and he was still in his corner. I asked how long he was in the shop, and the owner told me, he was there already for half a year, and nobody wanted to buy him because of his brown color."

An impulse buy? No.

Ellen did what any thoughtful person would do. "I went to the library and read a pet manual about rats," she said. "I went back to the shop, after reading about how smart and sweet they are, and bought him!"

One rat? Not enough for Ellen.

"To make a long story short," she said, "in another shop I bought him a friend, and they lived very happily together. I was getting used to them, and thought they were the most sweet animals."

When I asked how she got them to pose she confessed, "I put vanilla pudding on the musical instruments. They have a good memory, I think, so after a few times they remembered what I wanted them to do."

She added, "They are also very intelligent. I have to be fast in taking photos and have to be patient sometimes."

I know what she means. When I tried to take photos of my always-busy Iris, mostly what I got was a blur of action.

Jessica Florence, who lives in England, solved this problem. Many of her wonderful photos are of her rats fast asleep.

They're snoozing in piles with other rats, or in piles with stuffed animals, or napping under covers. My favorite may be Jessica's picture on page 114 of two rats on top of each other, holding a teddy bear. There's something about seeing their hands, the delicate and dainty nails at the end of long fingers, that makes us read ourselves into her photos. *That could be me. That could be my baby. That could be someone I love.*

When I asked her about her life with rats, Jessica revealed that she had to be persistent at first:

> I first got a pet rat when I was thirteen after my parents finally relented to my begging. I had seen a rat on a TV show which was testing various pets' intelligence and I fell in love with the creatures instantly. I then had eleven rats over the course of the following eight years. I've been without rats for the last two years due to the fact I was busy with my new son, but now that he is two I will be getting two new females in the coming weeks. I'm very excited about that!
>
> The photographs came about because I had discovered a new interest in photography at the time and I had no human models that would pose for me. It was actually a last resort that I began

photographing my then pet rat, Bug. But the photos took off online and I started to really enjoy photographing her. She was very easy to pose and the ideal model really.

It's nice that I am still so associated with rats online, because they are animals I am really passionate about and I love changing the odd person's opinion about them. The best thing is when I get emails from those who have been inspired to get pet rats themselves because of the photos.

Don't forget that Jessica is British. When she says "the odd person's opinion," I think she means the random person. Not a weirdo who doesn't like rats. Though that might be what she means.

With her photos Jessica is on to something important here. It's hard for anyone to look threatening when sleeping. We are at our most vulnerable and unguarded when we're asleep. If Jessica's photographs don't make you think rats are adorable, I give up.

Actually, I don't. Not yet.

I'm going to keep trying to convert you. And to do that, I'll refer you to a teen from Philadelphia who has wowed the world with her YouTube video "15 Incredible Rat Tricks."

Abby Roeser taught her rats Nami and Pepper a bunch

of tricks. As one of over a million viewers, I have spent time I couldn't afford to waste watching them perform the following tricks: spin, fetch, hurdle jump, open the cabinet by pulling a string, jump into Abby's hand, circle around an object, scoot a ball along a wire, dive underwater for peas, go through a hoop, weave around an obstacle course, untie Abby's shoe, roll over, do the laundry (put tiny "socks" into a tiny "washing machine"), perform a dramatic teddy-bear rescue, and play doctor by opening a first-aid kit, removing a Band-Aid, and bringing it to Abby.

After I watched Abby's videos I wondered if Iris would have enjoyed learning tricks. I never bothered teaching her anything. She did her own thing—like twirling for broccoli and coming when I clapped and called her name. Mostly I just wanted her company, snuggling with me when I watched TV, sleeping on my lap when I sat at my computer, resting against a book when I lay in bed reading. I spend a lot of time reading.

Why, I wondered, were there no good books with rats as the main characters? I mean, after all, *rats* spelled backward is *star*.

Mice, small and unthreatening, often appear in children's books. Like kids, they are easily squished and need protection. But it's rare a rat is the hero.

Think about one of the most famous literary rats. Templeton, from *Charlotte's Web*, is hard to like. The author, E. B. White, writes, "The rat had no morals, no conscience, no scruples, no consideration, no decency, no milk of rodent kindness, no compunctions, no higher feeling, no friendliness, no anything." Not exactly the hero I'm looking for.

You'd think that Beatrix Potter, lover of rodents, creator of Peter Rabbit, a woman who dedicated *The Tale of Samuel Whiskers or The Roly-Poly Pudding* to her own pet rat, Sammy, would have come through for us.

Sadly, no.

In that book, the title character is indeed a rat, but he's a snuff-taking, thieving, domineering old guy who, with his wife, tries to eat kittens.

And who could forget the most horrific rat-infested tale of all, that of the Pied Piper of Hamelin? In the poet Robert Browning's version, the town of Hamelin was in trouble:

> *Rats!*
> *They fought the dogs and killed the cats,*
> *And bit the babies in the cradles,*
> *And ate the cheeses out of the vats,*
> *And licked the soup from the cooks' own ladles,*

Split open the kegs of salted sprats,
Made nests inside men's Sunday hats,
And even spoiled the women's chats,
By drowning their speaking
With shrieking and squeaking
In fifty different sharps and flats.

In other words, these guys were simply doing what rats do—trying to stay alive. The townspeople hired the piper to lure the rats away. He did. He led them into the river, where they drowned. When the citizens refused to pay him for his services, the musician, dressed in his multicolored (pied) clothes, blew into his pipe and lured away the children. Horrors!

Even my idol, George Orwell, goes to the dark side when it comes to rats. In *1984*, the imprisoned hero Winston is threatened with a torture device straight out of his worst nightmares—a mask attached to a cage of "carnivorous" rats. Oh, George. Really. Did you have to go there?

Over the years, I've accumulated a big stack of books about rats. Far too many of them, in my opinion, are about plague. Or about the destruction rats cause, the havoc they can wreak.

In *More Cunning Than Man*, Robert Hendrickson writes,

> What is certain is that any history of the rat is a history of human misery. More numerous than man on earth, sustained by human food, living largely by human sloth, the dread black plagues that rats deliver have alone killed billions throughout history, more than all man's wars and revolutions combined. Rats are as deadly and fecund as germs; a single pair can potentially produce 359 million heirs in three years.

Okay. If you want to read that kind of thing, go to his book.

Jerry Langton devotes a chapter—well, almost a chapter —to the people who love their pet rats in his book *Rat: How the World's Most Notorious Rodent Clawed Its Way to the Top*. Langton reduces the "hundreds" of rat lovers in the world to a caricature—the tattooed and pierced outcast. Even as he realizes he's flattening the terrain of rat-ownership into a simple one-dimensional picture, he maintains this is true for *every one* of the people he met. For instance, he speaks to a rat owner named Maura, a young woman who keeps apologizing for referring to him as "normal," because she's not used to talking to people who are mainstream and are interested in rats.

No normal people, Langton implies, choose to live with rats.

Langton starts out by describing Maura in a way that seems oddly dismissive. He says she insists on being called "Raven," and he sizes her up as five feet three inches and about 260 pounds. (He feels her weight is important to mention—why?) He says that she has multiple piercings and keeps expecting him to be afraid of her rat.

> Like all other rat owners I've met, she [Raven] explains she likes rats because they are smart, affectionate, and clean. And, like all the others, she's adamant about these claims. Rat owners love to talk about their pets and use the word "extremely" more than any group of people I've ever met. Their rats are "extremely" clean, "extremely" affectionate, "extremely" intelligent, and "extremely" cute, among other extreme claims.

Even after claiming he hates to "paint an entire group with such a wide brush," he goes on to do just that. He describes the rat owners he's met—and he says he's talked to more than a hundred individuals—as eccentric and mis-understood, and their sense of being hated for no good reason is, he says, their reason for choosing rats as pets. Perhaps revealing more about himself than about his subject, he goes on to say,

> All had strong, usually antiestablishment, political views they were pleased to share. Many had tattoos, piercings, or other look-at-me adornments. Many expressed an interest in science fiction, fantasy and/or medieval times. Many were vegetarians.

Gotta watch out for those vegetarians.

In a book about rats, he devotes very few pages to representing the other side of the rats-are-vile-and-disgusting-creatures argument. Indeed, even in Raven's chapter, clearly unconvinced of the charms of both rats and their people, he scurries on to the topics of rat baiting and rat eating. He seems more eager to leave the company of the tattooed rat lovers than he did the sewers he crawled around in, filled with human feces, used condoms, and wild rats.

There are plenty of rat-care and even training guides—more on that later—but really, I've found only two novels that portray rats in their full humanity. One, published in 1986, is called *A Rat's Tale*. It is a delightful satire of New York social circles whose characters happen to be rats.

I was so enchanted by the book that I emailed the author, Tor Seidler, told him how much I loved the book and the gorgeous illustrations done by a famous artist and book designer, Fred Marcellino, and said that surely someone who was able to write a book that sees these critters for the kind, nurturing, brave, and industrious souls they are has had a rat friend or two.

Tor wrote back right away and explained,

> I never actually had a rat as a pet, but I did have a good friend with a white rat that I grew quite fond of. The impetus for writing *A Rat's Tale* came from jogging in Central Park. I used to live uptown and often ran around the reservoir. I would spot rats from time to time, particularly in the fall when you could hear them in the fallen leaves (no bushy squirrel tails). Then I started to notice flyers posted on trees advising dog owners to keep out of certain areas on account of rat poison. I felt for the rats. It seemed to me they were being unfairly persecuted.

My kind of guy! And a fellow runner! Tor also said rats appealed to him because he liked the idea of writing about an "uncuddly creature." He wrote, "Back then it seemed most anthropomorphic tales featured mice or rabbits or such."

It's true. Mice and bunnies are more often heroes in kids' books. As I said earlier, I think that's because mice and bunnies are small and defenseless and need looking out for. In other words, they're a lot like children. Rats, I think, are more like teenagers. They're bold and unafraid. They like to explore. They're eager to try new things. They're curious. They're physically tough. Sometimes they make mistakes and get themselves into trouble, but they're rarely malicious. They have big, strong hearts.

Among those in the know when it comes to rat-friendly books, there is one everyone mentions: Robert C. O'Brien's *Mrs. Frisby and the Rats of NIMH*. It's a book I'd never read, had heard of only in a vague sort of way, but it sounded sci-fi-ish and it was, after all, for children. In other words, not my kind of book.

Then I read it.

Mrs. Frisby is a widowed mouse. She goes in search of help for her ailing son, Timothy, who may be too weak for their seasonal move to escape the farmer's plow. *Here we go again*, I thought. Those mice always need to be safeguarded. And as with many animal fables, *Mrs. Frisby* has a cast of different critters around to help (crow, owl) and to threaten (cat). But when Mrs. Frisby gets to the rats things become interesting.

A rat named Nicodemus describes how he and his brethren lived happy, peaceful lives near a farmers' market. They created their own society and didn't bother or infringe on anyone else. The farmers left a wake of waste—the trimmings of meat and vegetables, the guts of fish—and so they had plenty of food and a good place to play: "There were empty boxes for hide-and-seek, there were walls to climb, tin cans to roll, and pieces of twine to tie and swing on. There was even, in the middle of the square, a fountain to swim in when the weather was hot."

One day people came in an odd white truck with the letters *NIMH* on it. The rats didn't pay much attention until men bearing nets captured them.

Researchers from the National Institute of Mental Health (NIMH) kidnapped Nicodemus and the others and enslaved them to science. The rats came to live in a way totally dissimilar to what they were used to. The scientists busted up the rats' family structures and forced them to live in solitary confinement, cut off from communication with one another and the world they knew. The rats were given new names, different from and simpler than the names they called themselves and one another. And the scientists subjected the rats to torture: a daily needle stick. While these captors were mostly benevolent, and the rats couldn't complain too much about their lives—they had housing, they had food, though not what they would have chosen to eat, nothing delicious—what they missed most was their freedom.

The experiment turned out to be about creating super-rats—the best specimens you could imagine. The drugs given to the first group, which included our hero, Nicodemus, and his closest friends, were designed to make the rats smarter and strong enough to beat the aging process. And they did. (Rats on 'roids—live strong, live long!) The experimenters began teaching the rats the basics of reading—recognizing letters and then putting them together into simple words, *RAT, CAT*. But the rats caught on more quickly than expected, and soon could read complicated sentences. They were shrewd enough not to give themselves away; like oppressed people everywhere they let perceived ignorance protect them. Allowing oneself to be underestimated has long been a strategy of the marginalized.

Once the rats of NIMH start learning to read, we can predict what will come next.

They are able to understand the instructions on their cages—"To release door, pull knob forward and slide right"—and figure out how to open them and ultimately escape.

The band of fugitive rats makes it to the outside world and is faced with a problem: "We don't know where to go because we don't know what we are." The big question is: "Where does a group of civilized rats fit in?"

Isn't that what each of us wonders at some point? *Where do I fit in?*

Here's my interpretation of *Mrs. Frisby and the Rats of NIMH*: it's a classic slave narrative and carries in it echoes of themes and events in Frederick Douglass's famous autobiography.

Huh?

For Douglass, as for the rats of NIMH, the path from slavery to freedom was literacy. Born on a slave plantation in 1817 or 1818, Douglass lived in the big house until he was seven, when his owner gave him away. His new mistress, Sophia Auld, had not been raised under the rigid rules of slavery and treated young Frederick more kindly than most slaves could expect. She even began to teach him to read, until her husband put a stop to it: educated slaves are unmanageable slaves, the argument went.

Eventually Sophia turned out to be as vile as her slave-owning husband, but twelve-year-old Frederick had learned enough to hatch a plan to get the white boys he met on the street to continue to teach him how to read. Ultimately Douglass grew into one of the great American stylists. Please do yourself a favor and get a copy of *Narrative of the Life of Frederick Douglass, an American Slave.* Then write me an email and tell me how much you loved it. I promise: you will love it.

The author of *Mrs. Frisby*, the magazine writer Robert Leslie Conly, published the book under the name Robert C. O'Brien. He may or may not have had in mind Frederick Douglass when he wrote it. But the capturing of the rats, the changing of their names and uprooting of their lives, the "benevolent" dictatorship of life in the laboratory, and the idea that the way out of this mess was through literacy strike me as similar to the narratives of many freed slaves. One of the great things about books is that we get not only to read them, but to read things into them. They become living objects apart from what the author intended.

Many readers believe Conly based his novel on the work of a scientist at the National Institute of Mental Health named John B. Calhoun. Again, the author may or may not have done that. He may have heard about Calhoun's work and it settled somewhere in his subconscious, and when he started to write, it sprang up, transformed and translated into something he could use. That's often the way the creative process works.

Regardless of whether or not the work was the basis for *Mrs. Frisby and the Rats of NIMH*, what Calhoun did is fascinating. He began to watch rats and in 1947 got his neighbor to agree to let him do research in a quarter-acre pen he called a "Garden of Eden." He designed a series of experiments to look at what happened to breeding under ideal or utopian conditions. As a scientist, he wanted to see what would happen when rats could breed in the presence of plentiful resources. Because rats are such baby-making machines, the colony could have expanded to five thousand. But for the two years he watched them, the population stayed around one hundred and fifty, never going higher than two hundred. The rats arranged themselves into living groups of ten to twelve.

Under natural circumstances, the population level managed to stay stable. But Calhoun wanted to know what would happen when they lived in more cramped quarters. What goes on when a bunch of critters are forced into uncomfortably close proximity?

Well, weird behavioral stuff went down. Some of the

swaggering boys formed gangs and attacked women and children. Mothers abandoned their kids. The misfits banded together and formed a sort of Breakfast Club. This group of rats, who had been picked on, withdrew from the larger society and got creative. In fact, they became artists and visionaries. When these rats dug in the dirt they didn't just leave messy piles around. Instead, they packed the dirt into a big ball and rolled it out of their area.

The way I've described Calhoun's experiments makes the rats sound pretty human. Calhoun did this himself. He personified and anthropomorphized his types of rats so we could readily recognize them: the females who chased after objects he called the "pied pipers," and the ones who groomed themselves obsessively he dubbed the "beautiful ones." He described "social dropouts" and "autistics." Members of the gangs of youngsters who attacked and pillaged he called "juvenile delinquents" and "probers."

Here's the big finding of Calhoun's early work: circumstances of overcrowding lead to what he called a "behavioral sink," where normal rules of good conduct wash down the drain. This, as you've already probably realized, became analogous to what happens when people live too closely together in cities.

In 1968, the great writer Tom Wolfe figured this topic

would make for a good magazine article. The essay, "O Rotten Gotham—Sliding Down into the Behavioral Sink," appears as the last chapter in his 1968 collection *The Pump House Gang*.

Where most writers might make the notion of overpopulation and urban blight seem dreary, Wolfe lights up the page: "I have just spent two days with Edward T. Hall, an anthropologist, watching thousands of my fellow New Yorkers short-circuit themselves into hot little twitching death balls with jolts of their own adrenaline."

The scientist Hall explains to Wolfe that it's overcrowding that does it, gets the adrenaline going. Wolfe reports, "And here they are, hyped up, turning bilious, nephritic, queer, autistic, sadistic, barren, batty, sloppy, hot-in-the-pants, chancred-on-the-flankers, leering, puling, numb—the usual in New York, in other words."

Wolfe and Hall stand on the balcony in Grand Central Terminal and look down: "The floor was filled with the poor white humans, running around, dodging, blinking their eyes, making a sound like a pen full of starlings or rats or something."

Dr. Hall had learned, of course, from Dr. Calhoun's rats, and had extrapolated the findings to describe the situation when many people live in too small a space. He also told the story of what happens after the population moves beyond the behavioral sink and goes to the next stage: collapse.

Calhoun never let his rats get to that point, but another researcher started observing related behavior among Sika deer on a small island off the Maryland shore. These deer each needed about three acres of space; the island was 280 acres. From an original group of four or five deer, they did what critters do and bred until they reached, in 1955, a herd of about three hundred. Suddenly, in 1958, more than half of them died. A year later even more perished, and the population leveled off at around eighty.

Here's the weird part: autopsies revealed that all the deer who died were healthy. They had plenty to eat and showed no signs of disease. The scientists found that living in overcrowded conditions caused deer to die of adrenaline overdose.

You might see how this kind of research could be used if applied to humans, especially humans who lived in overcrowded cities. The world wasn't thrilled to hear that overpopulation might cause people to behave badly and then die of stress.

In a scholarly article on Calhoun's work, "Escaping the Laboratory: The Rodent Experiments of John B. Calhoun and Their Cultural Influence," two economists, Edmund

Ramsden and Jon Adams, claim Calhoun didn't get a fair shake. Because his early work on the bad effects of over-crowding captured the imagination of writers like Tom Wolfe and the public, it is only his pessimistic conclusions that are remembered. But Calhoun never thought human-ity was doomed to wallow in a behavioral sewer. Once we understood the problem, he believed we could seek to find a way to solve it—to start a revolution in the way we live. As the authors of the article write, "Everyone wants to hear the diagnosis, no one wants to hear the cure."

I know, it's a long way from *Ratatouille* to *Mrs. Frisby* to slavery to population science to a writer like Tom Wolfe, but I learned from Iris the importance of being able to jump around.

Iris, the poochiesnoggins honeymunchkin

Mistakes Were Made

What should you know before you get a rat?

I had moved to Missoula, Montana, to go to graduate school, and for the first time in my life I lived alone.

I'd lost Hannah, my dog of nearly eighteen years. No one—no creature—could take her place. I wasn't ready for another pet. My future was uncertain. After graduate school, where would I go? What would I do? And so I came home at the end of the day with no one to tell it to. I woke in the morning and didn't use my voice. I carried nuts with me so I could buy the friendship of anonymous squirrels on the street.

Whenever I'd visit my friend Dan at his small ranch

nestled between the Bitterroot and the Sapphire Mountains, where he lived among a loving masculine posse of a dog, a cat, and two geldings, he'd watch as I played with his critters and then look at me without understanding.

"You need a pet," he'd say.

Missoula is a dog-friendly town, my friend Judy would remind me each time I went to dinner at her house. "Why don't you get a dog?" she'd ask as her two cats wound around my feet or I picked them up to bury my face in their long, soft fur.

I started dating a guy who had a wolf. Yes, in Montana there are guys who have wolves. But neither the wolf nor the man filled the Hannah-shaped hole in my heart.

While skimming through the *Norton Book of Nature Writing*, I came across an essay called "Mouse." It's a small, quiet piece by Faith McNulty, who was a nature writer for the *New Yorker*. She and her husband find a baby mouse and take her into their home and hearts. McNulty lovingly describes her tiny rodent.

I read the essay and figured out how to fix my life.

Mice are sweet and delightful, but rats are clever and have a better sense of humor. I know. I've loved both. I knew I wanted another rat.

I called a local pet store and learned they had no rats in stock.

Would they be getting them?

Call back the following week, I was told. When I did, the man on the phone, the manager, assured me a shipment would be coming in on Thursday. The rats would be young—four or five weeks old. They'd cost $4.99 each.

I went to the pet store. It was in a mall. The guy I'd spoken with turned out to be named Steve. Weedy and hunched, he had what can only be called a "molestache"— neither ironic nor hip, a sad tuft of fur lodged above his upper lip. I worried about picking out a rat and wondered if I could trust a guy with such bad taste in his own facial hair. I've been known to choose both well and terribly when it comes to men. I wasn't sure how good my judgment would be in selecting a rat.

In the glass aquarium a handful of baby rats skittered around while others slept in a pile. I told Steve I wanted a female. I generally prefer female animals; I know how testosterone can work as a drug. And also, well, have you seen a full-grown male rat? People tend to get hung up on the tail when it comes to rats, but have you ever seen, ahem, rat balls? They're ginormous. If a rat were a man, it would look like he had cantaloupes for testicles.

Steve plucked a tiny baby by the tail, checked the junk, and put him back. He picked up a pretty blond-and-white girl. She pooped. And then pooped and pooped. I said no.

Not because I have anything against poop, but because rats poop when they are distressed. I didn't want a high-strung rat. That girl was a drama queen.

He grabbed another calm-seeming black-and-white number. Rat balls. He put him back.

I pointed Steve toward a small girl. When he picked her up, she sat in his hand and looked around. Then, contented and unruffled, she started cleaning herself. That's her, I said.

He boxed her up like a Happy Meal while I purchased some rat food, a cage, bedding, and some ill-advised toys, including an exercise wheel, which she never once ran on. (Her mother's rat: I hate treadmills, too.) Excited and scared, I could not wait to get her home.

As we drove out of the parking lot, I stuck a finger through one of the holes in the box and let her sniff me, felt her soft tongue on my skin. And then I felt a bump. A big bump.

Oops.

I had driven into the car in front of me.

A woman got out, came around, and set about examining her bumper. I sat in my car, trying to make sure the baby rat hadn't been upset by the accident.

I put down my window and said sorry. I told her I'd just gotten a baby rat. I may even have said something like, "She's adorable! Do you want to see her?"

At that point, excited about the new addition to my family, I wasn't even thinking about things like exchanging car insurance information or enormous body shop bills I couldn't afford.

The woman held up her hands and said, "No problem, no problem," and hurried back to her uninjured car. She clearly wanted to get away from the crazy rat lady.

I watched her dart into her vehicle and drive off. I reassured my tiny passenger that everything was fine and put my fingers near the holes in the box.

When we got back to my apartment I let the baby rat run around on the floor. Timid at first, she planted her rear feet in one place and then reached out with her forepaws and nose to sniff and explore. I had planned to name her Frieda, after a Montanan I'd been doing research on, a strong, independent woman involved in politics and the arts, someone I admired. I believe in giving animals human names. I could no more call a pet something like Fancy, or Brownie, or Sparky than I could imagine saddling a child with one of those humiliating names. Though in truth, I wouldn't mind being called Sparky.

But when I looked at this tiny creature I didn't see a Frieda. I figured I'd wait and soon enough the right name would come to me.

And soon enough it did. From the spine of a novel in a stack on the floor that my new pet was investigating. Iris. Iris Murdoch was an English novelist and philosopher, a professor at Oxford University. I'd read one of her novels my freshman year in college and had loved her ever since. My rat would be Iris.

It was Valentine's Day. I had chosen to spend it getting a pet rather than with my wolf-owning boyfriend. To his credit he later said, "I knew my days were numbered when you got the rat."

Before any of the real rat experts reading this can get their knickers in a knot, let me just say I know things now I didn't know then.

I realize how many bullets I dodged.

Picking out a rat from a cage where the boys and the girls live and play together is not a good idea. Iris was probably days away from reaching sexual maturity. I wanted one rat, not a dozen. Many females come from pet stores to their new homes knocked up.

Iris turned out to be healthy. (And thankfully not pregnant.) I got her young enough that she became accustomed to being held and handled by me; older rats sometimes don't adjust as well when they've spent their entire lives in cages with little human contact, though it's hard to find a rat who can't be won over by some TLC.

When you get rats from pet stores you might need to do a lot of caring for them: they are often sick. You don't know how old they are or where they've been or what they've been exposed to or how they've been treated.

I wanted a girl because I didn't like the look of rat testicles. What I didn't know then is that female rats lead busy lives. When she wasn't sleeping or cuddled up with me, Iris had a lot to do. She would go on reconnaissance missions. She'd greet everyone who came into the house. *(Plumber! The plumber's here!)* She collected stuff. I'd find stashes of tissues and tiny objects in corners of the closet and on top of books. When I offered Iris food, she'd take it and run off to stockpile it somewhere.

The problem with living with someone who has an active mind and a restless nature, as anyone who's ever lived with me can attest, is that when they're bored, they go looking for trouble. Iris would often want to play while I worked. She'd box with my fingers as I typed on the computer. She'd place herself between me and my book. She'd race back and forth on the bed. If I wanted only a cuddle bunny, I should have picked a male. But I'm a big fan of study breaks. When Iris wanted to play, I'd play.

I had read enough to know not to get pine or cedar shavings for bedding, since those woods emit volatile compounds that can be toxic to rats. Instead I paid money I didn't have as a starving graduate student to buy fluffy CareFRESH recycled-paper litter to line her cage.

The soon-to-be-dumped boyfriend bought her a wooden sleeping hut, a gesture that made me appreciate him, but not enough to keep him around. She loved her hut and I loved that memory of his kindness.

The bulk of Iris's diet consisted of rat pellets, blocks of something that didn't seem much like food but that she found quite delicious. Now I know many rat parents who make their darlings' food by combining nuts, seeds, cereal, Pirate's Booty, whatever.

Look. I know what you're thinking. I was a bad rat mama.

Here's what you have to understand. The staples of my diet are Cheez-Its, Tootsie Rolls, and diet A&W root beer. If it can't be microwaved, I don't eat it. I made sure the munchkin had plenty of organic broccoli (a bit of chemical goes a long way when you weigh only as much as a Snickers bar) and shared whatever real food I ate with her. Even if she'd just eaten nothing but rat pellets, I'm pretty sure her diet would have been healthier and better balanced than mine. (I know, that's not saying much.)

Iris's cage was the equivalent of the one-bedroom apartment we lived in then, nothing like the multistoried rat mansions I've seen. It was simple, with a couple of shelves, and she was in it only at bedtime. I knew I wasn't supposed to keep it on the floor because that could be drafty, but I also wanted to keep the door open when I was home so she could come and go as she pleased. I built her a staircase of books. She climbed on *Paradise Lost*, *Middlemarch*, and *Ulysses* to get in and out of her cage.

Now, one thing the rat people are adamant about is that you should never have just one rat. It honestly never occurred to me to get more than one. I am a serial monogamist. I've only ever had one animal (and one boyfriend) at a time. That's how I roll.

Some rat fans will argue that keeping Iris without a rodent companion was like sending her to the hole for life. Breeders, authors of rat-care websites and books, teenagers on rat Facebook groups, basically all manner of animal lovers will be quick to skewer me for this. They will say things like, "Rats are social animals and need to be with others of their kind." They will say things like, "Rats who live alone will become withdrawn and may develop behavioral problems." They will write on their websites, "Why on earth would anyone settle for just one rat when they could have two!?!"

I'm not dismissing their concerns. Indeed, you can find plenty of authoritative support for this position. According to *The Laboratory Rat*, a textbook for veterinarians and researchers who use animals, "It is nearly impossible to keep a single rat happy, even if you are especially conscientious about handling it regularly throughout the day. A rat needs almost constant interaction to prevent boredom, so if you only have one, you become the animal's main source of social stimulation."

No one who ever met Iris would describe her as withdrawn or unhappy. She was perhaps the cheeriest, most well-adapted being I've ever met. If you don't believe me, you can call anyone on her long list of friends as a witness. I'll give you their numbers.

The fact is, I don't like blanket rules. I believe in individual difference, that a one-size-fits-all approach generally doesn't fit. What works for you—or your rat—may not work for me.

Because of my teaching schedule (lots of time at home) and my lackluster social life (lots of time at home), Iris spent more hours out of her cage than she did in it. She probably thought of me as a big dumb rat she had to look out for. She'd go off on her household explorations but come back periodically to check on me. If one of us worried more about the other, I'd guess she would be the one with a furrowed brow.

The only time I thought it would have been better to have two rats was when I had to travel. I couldn't leave Iris alone. That would have been abuse. So I made sure that when I went out of town she had plenty of human companionship: I lined up a crew of rat sitters who came to love the little munchkin almost as much as I did.

Like littermates, Iris and I groomed each other. She found specks of dirt under my fingernails and cleaned them gently away with her teeth. When I got out of the shower, she licked the lower parts of my legs dry. And even though she was a champion of personal hygiene, she often neglected her tail. When her tail got dirty, I'd fill up the sink with warm water and a few drops of shampoo and give her a bath. I scrubbed her tail and massaged her tiny body clean and conditioned her fur. Afterward, I'd wrap her in a washcloth like a burrito and towel her off. Then I'd blow-dry her on low and she'd emerge a fluffy, delicious-smelling varmint.

For exercise, we chased each other around my apartment. Mostly Iris chased me. She tended to follow me everywhere. When I clapped my hands and called her name, she'd come running from wherever she was. Sometimes I'd be wandering around looking for her, clapping my hands and saying her name, and finally I'd turn and Iris would be staring up at me. I could see her thinking, "I'm right here! What are you going on about?" After the first couple of weeks it was clear that in my apartment 1) there was nowhere for her to go, and 2) she preferred to be with me than to be alone. So when I was home, we had an open-door policy and she rarely stayed in her cage.

Each morning I'd wake early, well before I needed to get up, open Iris's door, and then go into the bathroom to pee. Then I'd get back into bed. Iris would find her way to her litter box so she, too, could pee, and then she'd come into bed with me. What she'd do is run at a gallop from the living room, pass the bathroom, and fling herself at the quilt that hung from the bed down to the floor. She'd be able to get up a third of the way with one leap, then, hand over tiny hand, she'd shimmy to the summit. She'd pause at the foot of the bed, assess the situation, then come bounding over.

Rats have lots of different gaits. When uncertain, Iris would keep her back feet planted and stretch her body out far in front of her. She'd creep her front paws forward, getting so long you couldn't believe it.

She'd also do a fast trot. Sometimes she'd gallop. Sometimes she'd bound, a series of flying leaps across time and space. After she summited, she usually bounded. Right to me. She'd snuggle in, sometimes under the covers, sometimes not, and we'd doze.

I never let Iris sleep with me at night because I feared,

obviously, that I'd crush her. But I did let her come into bed early in the morning. And we napped together in the afternoon. And right until I turned out the light to go to sleep, she stayed by my side. Or on top of my legs. Or tucked under my chin. We were each other's pack.

At the end of graduate school I had to give a public reading. My mother couldn't make the trip, but my brother came from West Virginia with Eva, his three-year-old daughter, my friend Candace flew in from Maine, and my ex-boyfriend Mike trekked all the way from North Carolina. They were my family, a family I'd made.

I couldn't wait to introduce Iris to my peeps. Candace loved her immediately. Mike was characteristically more skeptical. When he'd first met Hannah, my dog, he said, "Where I come from, dogs live outside." Mike hails from a small town in Minnesota and has a physicist's blunt touch in describing reality as he sees it. We made a joke out of that comment for the next twenty years, especially as he soon grew to see Hannah as a member of his family. While theoretically interested in Iris, Mike carries with him the incredulity that accompanies the scientist personality. He'd never before met a rat and needed to be convinced by the evidence of her awesomeness.

Candace and Mike took control of fixing the food for the

reading while I milled around, nervous and distracted. I don't love reading my work in public. It's one of the things that come with the job of being a writer, but like most writers, I prefer to be behind my computer typing instead of standing in front of a bunch of people and stumbling over my own words.

At some point, a couple of hours before the event, I realized I hadn't seen Iris in a while. Mike and Candace sliced and cubed big blocks of Costco-bought cheese and chopped carrots in the kitchen. In my small apartment, the kitchen was separated from the living room by only a counter. Before I'd brought Iris home the first time, I'd checked thoroughly and found no escape routes. After I'd had her for a few days, I realized she would no more try to escape than I would kick her out.

But then, gone girl. I paced the small space clapping my hands and saying, in more and more frantic tones, "Iris, Iris, Iris." Candace and Mike joined in the search, then we kept running into one another (it was a very small apartment) and they went back to chopping.

And I lost it.

My rat was gone. My life was over. How could I have gotten so attached in such a short amount of time? We'd had only a few months together. I hadn't even realized how much I loved and needed her until she left. How could she leave?

The clock ticked. I had to get ready to go and read from my thesis. Mike and Candace knew me well enough to stay clear. The apartment was too tiny for the three of us and my enormous mass of anxiety. I went outside.

My friend Jason drove by to find me sitting on the curb, upset beyond consolation. I explained that I'd lost my rat. Jason, a good friend, asked if there was anything he could do. I shook him off, walked around the block a few times, and then went back upstairs.

I had hoped Iris would magically appear in my absence. She hadn't.

I thought about canceling the reading. Would that mean I couldn't graduate? Would I be laughed out of town?

Just before I had to leave, as we stood around the apartment and my friends tried to comfort me, Iris staggered out from under the couch, still drunk from sleep. She stopped a few feet away and let out a huge yawn, and then bounded over to me.

But, but, but . . . I'd looked behind the couch.

I'd looked under the couch.

She must have found a way to crawl up into it, something she'd never done before. I wondered if, with so many new people around and so much commotion, she just needed a quiet place to nap.

I smothered her with kisses and she indulged me until she'd had enough, and then, like a toddler, put up a tiny paw to fend off my lips. I brought her with me to the reading (yes, the owner allowed me to bring my rat into the restaurant), and though when I got up to read from my thesis she stayed in her travel cage, she spent the rest of the time on my shoulder, basking in the attention and greeting friends and strangers.

Mike was mad at her. He later said he thought she was a little stinker, hiding out and letting me worry.

Candace had a different take: "I remember thinking that I had seen you upset many times before, but when Iris went missing, you went to a place I had never seen you go. You went to the place that every mother goes to when her child is missing. It is a singular and sickening place."

Ready to roll

On the Road

What's it like to travel with a rat?

For the previous two years I had been thinking a lot about loss.

One morning, just after school had started, as I walked across the bridge that goes over the river that runs through the town of Missoula, I called my mother. When she answered, I said, as usual, "Hullo, it's me," and expected her to answer, "Hello, Me."

But that day I heard no play in her voice.

"I've got something to tell you."

My mother tended to flick on her warning blinker long before making a turn. She did this while driving, and in conversations. Like most of us, she had a hard time delivering bad news, so she telegraphed impending doom well in advance of conveying any real information. It could be anything from "I accidentally threw out the stinky old running shoes you left here" to "A tree fell on the house."

I'd just reached the bridge. I looked down at the rocks, and as always happened to me in Missoula, lines from Norman Maclean's beautiful book *A River Runs Through It* bubbled in my head:

> Eventually, all things merge into one, and a river runs through it. The river was cut by the world's great flood and runs over rocks from the basement of time. On some of the rocks are timeless raindrops. Under the rocks are the words, and some of the words are theirs.

I glanced down at the swift current flowing over ancient rocks as my mom said, "I have some bad news."

Still water is quiet, restful. Moving water is noisy. It's one of the reasons I don't like the ocean. Too unruly, too loud. The sound of the river combined with cars going by made it hard to hear. I listened to the gurgles and rush as my mother talked, explaining.

Back pain she assumed had been from a car accident a year before.

Trips to visit doctors.

Misdiagnosis.

Oncologist.

Multiple myeloma.

Cancer of the blood.

Incurable.

Five to ten years.

Fatal.

After the call ended, I walked over the bridge and sat by the side of the river with my head in my hands. As a kid I had a recurring dream that my mother was tied to a chair sunk at the deep end of a swimming pool. I'd dive in and try to untie her but I could never manage it. I'd wake gasping for breath, crying. Nothing I could imagine would be worse than watching my mother suffer and not being able to save her.

When I told her about this dream decades later, she said, "You saw it."

I said, "Saw what?"

"That I was drowning in my marriage."

I'm not sure I saw that, but worries about my mother never left me. Every child knows she is likely to outlive her parents; the prospect of loss is always there, even if we try not to think about it.

When you get a rat, you know you will have her for about a thousand days. That's it. From the moment I got Iris as a tiny baby I wanted to slow time. I made sure to enjoy each minute I had with her because I knew how quickly they would pass. With beloved parents, even though you know they will die, you can't afford to let yourself think about it.

For the next two years I spent every vacation traveling through four airports on three flights for thirteen hours to get from Missoula, Montana, to Ithaca, New York. Each morning as I walked to school I called and talked to the woman I called the CLM, the Cute Little Mother.

At first we talked about the medicine. She had her doctor send me charts and lab tests, and I talked them over with friends in the cancer business. I got names of specialists and developed my own ideas about treatment options. I never fully accepted the notion that even if I found out what the "right" thing to do was, it wouldn't matter unless I could convince her of it. I had a hard time allowing my mother to be the master of her own body, her own fate.

Two years after her diagnosis, when I had finished grad school and nabbed a job as a professor in Spokane, Washington, I decided to spend the summer with my mother and stepfather in upstate New York. For me, as was the case for Odysseus, that epic Greek hero, getting back to Ithaca wasn't such an easy feat. I had to drive because I couldn't fly. More precisely, Iris couldn't fly. The airlines had an idiotic rule, a rule that is at bottom bigoted and, like all bigotry, based on ignorance and fear. Rats can't fly.

Dogs, cats, and birds can go under the seat in front of you. Hamsters, those porky terrorists from the Mideast who look cute and cuddly, but are short, nasty, and brutish creatures, can fly in the cargo hold. So can guinea pigs. But mice and rats are not accepted in the friendly skies. Iris could not fly, so we had to drive across the country.

I am not a good driver. Though I am an endurance athlete and regularly run marathons and races even longer than 26.2 miles, I am able to go no more than three or four hours behind the wheel before I begin to drift off and am wakened by the sound of my car's wheels zipping over the rumble strip. Iris and I were not fit to make the trip back east on our own.

My friend Andrew is one of the funniest people I know and he has saved many of my days. We used to date and now we're just friends. I told him about my problem; he said we would work something out. He had to give a talk in Chicago a few days after I had to leave for my big drive. He could, he said, fly to Spokane and drive with me as far as Chicago, where I could stop to hang out with my college roommate Val and her family. Then I could drive the rest of the way on my own. A great plan.

So we three hit the road: a rat, a psychiatrist, and me.

Let me tell you some things about Andrew. He's interested in everything from stinky cheese to the origins of the universe. He's a total geek and the most gifted natural athlete I've ever met. He's always late because he agrees to do too many things and he can never catch up. I used to try to fine him a quarter for every minute he kept me waiting, but he was perfectly happy to hand over cash and not even try to reform.

He'd gotten married not long before. When his wife, Ellen, heard Andrew was thinking of driving across the country with me, she said to him, "You're a really good friend. I admire you for doing that." We called her a lot from the road to tell her how much we adored and appreciated her. Often when we called we both bellowed out at once, talking over each other, raving like lunatics. She took it, as she does everything, in stride.

Iris was, of course, thrilled to meet Andrew. *New person!* And Andrew was kind and gentle with her. He tended to show his love with food and I had to keep him from overfeeding her. Andrew was a spoiler, which turned me into the strict one, a role I did not love. But neither did I want an obese animal. So Andrew would plead to give Iris treats and I'd say no. He'd beg and I'd give in and say, "Small and healthy! Small and healthy!"

In the car Iris spent a lot of time on my lap. Sometimes she'd explore the floor near my feet. Andrew would want to pet her and talk to her and I'd have to gently remind him to PAY ATTENTION TO THE ROAD OR YOU'RE GOING TO KILL US ALL!

Andrew realized he had three medical journal articles due or past due. So after we'd spent some time catching up on gossip, had a couple of small spats about where to get gas, and had given Iris plenty of attention and pieces of broccoli, we got to work. He drove. I had his computer on my lap. A half-eaten bag of Kettle Korn rested between us.

I started to read his manuscripts, and then asked a few simple questions: "How did you manage to graduate from such fancy-pants schools if you can't even write a sentence?" "Do you know what a sentence is?" "This is a comma"— wild body gesture from the passenger seat here—"learn what it does! You can't just sprinkle them on your prose like salt."

Whenever I ask Andrew to explain his medical work to me—something I do frequently—I am captivated. He has the ability to get at the most interesting issues, to draw out the implications of what he's studying, and to explain ideas in fascinating ways. He knows how to tell a story. He knows which details will enhance suspense, which will come as a surprise.

But when it comes to putting it on the page, those skills mysteriously desert him. He writes in simple, declarative, passive sentences. He endlessly repeats words and phrases. He has no idea how commas and paragraph breaks can be your friends, that adverbs are the refuge of the weak and lazy, and that semicolons, like loaded guns, should only be handled by those who are trained to use them.

He drove, I edited, and Iris slept in her cage or on my shoulder or nestled in my lap. On one of the manuscripts I added my name as co-author, and inserted lavish acknowledgments into the text: "Rachel is the most totally awesome and inspiring person in the whole world and without her (and the wonderful Iris) Andrew would be lost." *That should teach him the value of proofreading his work*, I thought.

We wanted to make it to Deadwood the first day—about eleven hours of drive time. Actually, I wanted to make it to Deadwood, having become addicted to the HBO series of the same name from years back that showed the dark, gritty settlement history of the West. Andrew had never seen the program, and asked why I kept calling him a name that should probably not be printed in a book like this. Nothing personal, I explained; on the show, every other word is c#$ks%*@$r.

I had stocked up on audio books I thought we'd both enjoy. Iris had tortillas and organic broccoli. We humans had the delicious Kettle Korn that was quickly finding its way all over the seats and floor, cookies, candy, peanut-butter-filled pretzels, berries (an Andrew favorite, which quickly became soupy and started to ferment in the triple-digit heat of a summer car and which he would not let me throw out), and some cucumbers that never got eaten.

Andrew had recently published a big drug study that was getting lots of media attention. He had heaps of requests for interviews. He told me he would have to take some calls on his cell while he drove.

"You don't understand," I said. "You can't count on having cell phone reception. We're driving through empty space."

He said we could stop at a gas station with a pay phone. Was he kidding?

Until you've driven across the country you might not have a sense of the desolation of the mountains, the vastness of the plains, the scarcity of gas stations.

Andrew didn't believe we weren't going to find a pay phone until we'd driven for many miles.

We had to stop in Bozeman, Montana, a bustling town infested with transplanted Californians and plenty of good restaurants, so Andrew could take his phone calls from radio stations.

I brought Iris into the restaurant in her travel cage, nestled in a canvas tote bag. I sneaked pieces of my sandwich to her. Andrew explained his research to the radio hosts while I made faces and motioned for him to hurry up.

We drove through Montana. We drove through a portion of Wyoming. We made it to South Dakota and decided to detour to see the big faces of the presidents on Mount Rushmore. "Meh," we said. We loved the Badlands, especially when we saw the prairie dog towns. I said we couldn't get out of the car because I knew those cute critters carried plague. Andrew didn't believe me and got out of the car. We had a fight in the parking lot, and an older couple in an RV gave us a knowing look and said, "Been traveling long?"

Finally we got to Deadwood.

"Keep driving," I said.

"Why?"

"This isn't right."

It looked like a neon, Disneyfied version of an old mining town. Busloads of tourists milled around the narrow main street. Casinos (there are casinos all over the West) advertised steak specials and discounts for tour groups.

"Keep driving," I said again to Andrew, and he did. We sped along for three more miles and stopped in Lead. (I learned much later it's pronounced *leed*, not *led*.) Lead looked like what I thought Deadwood should be: a tiny, tired old western town.

We ate a spectacularly bad meal at a restaurant, found a hotel, and complained to each other about not having Internet access.

Iris, who had been in and out of her cage during the drive, ran around on the big hotel beds. Then, as we all do after a long day's drive, she crashed. She fell asleep in Andrew's hand as he sat on a red velvet bench (redolent of a bordello) watching a Russell Crowe movie on cable. He'd held his hand out in an awkward way, letting Iris play. She played, and then fell asleep. Andrew didn't want to disturb her, so he sat and watched TV with his arm stretched out at an uncomfortable angle of repose, his hand filled with sleeping rat.

I told him she'd be fine if he moved her or put her back in her cage.

He wouldn't budge.

I asked if he'd seen the way rats sleep together—in big piles, stepping on one another's heads.

Nothing mattered to him. His arm got sore and his hand fell asleep, but he felt strongly that the little pumpkin remain peaceful.

This is the sort of thing that used to annoy me about Andrew. Then I remembered his deep store of empathy. Even though he would keep me waiting and make jokes that would go on for days, Andrew was one of the kindest, most compassionate men I knew. He saw himself in Iris and treated her as he'd like to be treated. That's a good way to live.

Andrew, Iris, and I made it to Chicago after many hours in the car, too much sugary food, and lots of squealing and complaining (from me). Then Iris and I left Andrew in Chicago so he could deliver a speech and, after spending the night with Val and her family, we continued our drive to upstate New York.

I knew that as much as I loved my mother, I couldn't spend the summer living with her. I was a grown-up, for Pete's sake, or at least I was when I was not around my family. The thing you never believe is that no matter how old you are, when you're with your parents you revert to the brattiest version of yourself. I knew this and tried to guard against it. I needed my own place. I wanted to be there for my sick mother, to take care of her, and also have space of my own. I had done some online poking around before I left and found a place—a room in a house—I thought would work.

When I got to Ithaca, I spent two nights in that room and realized it wouldn't work. The house was so hot Iris laid herself flat on her belly and didn't want to move. The guy who owned the home seemed, well, weird if not downright creepy.

On day three, Iris and I moved in with my mother and George, my stepfather.

When I'd first suggested that Iris and I spend that summer in upstate New York, my mother fussed and worried. Her immune system was compromised; could a rat make her sick?

To be fair, my mother appreciated animals and I'd grown up with a menagerie: a dog named Barkus whom I referred to as my sister; two tabby cats, a gray one named Ishtar and an orange guy with six toes I named Daedalus; Wilbur, a rabbit who did card tricks and loved Barkus, following her around and humping her tail; a mouse named Moosie who hated men and loved to have her cheek stroked; and Ophelia, a hamster who ate her own babies. My mom was not antianimal, but since she'd divorced my father when my brother left for college, she hadn't lived with any and had grown accustomed to maintaining a clean and tidy house. Once she got sick she couldn't bear any more responsibility.

I had to ask several doctors to reassure my mom that having a rat in the house would not endanger her health. It didn't help when I pointed out that Iris was kinder, had a better sense of humor, and smelled nicer than my brother, Mark. (No matter how old you get, sibling rivalry dies hard. He's really not so bad, but I was trying to make a point.)

And so, Iris and I moved in with my mother and George for the summer. At that point, my mom was very sick. Most days she couldn't do more than lie on the couch. I surveyed the house, but knew I didn't have to worry about letting Iris roam free. She would want to be with me, or with whoever else was around. We put her cage in my mother's office, where, before she'd gotten sick, my mom had spent days in front of her computer, writing books on graphic design and keeping up with her business of creating posters and logos for clients. Since she'd gotten sick she'd been able to spend less time at her desk and logged lots of hours on the living room couch, lying under a fleece blanket and reading.

And that's where Iris spent most of that summer: curled up on my mother's chest, between her chin and a library book.

When I let Iris out of her cage in my mother's house she

would do her usual floor patrol, conducting reconnaissance of seldom-used corners and performing surveillance under the table. But she always ended up in the living room.

Iris would charge across the floor, run along one of the L-shaped couches, traverse the end table, and leap onto my mother's neck. If I saw it in time I'd shout out, "INCOMING!" (No one likes to be startled, even by a ballistic missile of love.) Iris would push the novel out of the way to sniff gingerly at my mother's face.

My mother fretted. She worried. Iris had tiny needle-sharp claws and sometimes she would scratch my mother's thin skin. She liked to grab my mother's lips. Mom would push her away but Iris would not be deterred. She would crawl onto her neck.

It didn't take long before my mother started pointing out how cute Iris looked when she was sleeping. When I tried to clear away my mother's lunch plate, she would stop me and say, "Don't take that!"

"You're finished! There's nothing left."

"I'm saving those for Iris."

Sure enough, after each meal Mom piled up tiny pieces of tortilla, or cheese, or lumps of mashed potatoes for Iris and doled them out to her. Sometimes Iris would raise a tiny paw to my mother's lips as a thank-you. And then Iris would settle onto my mother's chest and there the two of them would remain for hours. I'd walk in on their conversations. I'd hear my mother talking to Iris, telling her how beautiful she was, what a good girl, and how much she loved her. Iris would grind her teeth in pleasure like a purring cat.

One night I went for dinner with a friend.

Iris had been out of her cage and wandering around the house, as usual. My mother and George were sitting in the living room watching a movie. At some point, one of them realized they didn't know where their grandrat was. After a while, their panic mounting, I got a phone call.

"Iris has disappeared."

I said, "Don't worry, she's probably sleeping somewhere." I thought about the time she had gone AWOL before my graduate reading.

"She'll turn up," I said. I worried for about seventeen seconds and then went back to my friend. She'd reappear soon. She always did.

When I got home, my mother and George were fairly frantic. They'd looked everywhere.

I searched the house. I knew Iris sometimes liked to go into my bed and crawl under the covers, and because she was so little she didn't make much of a lump and could be hard to find. I ran my hands over all the blankets. Not there. She didn't like to be on the floor, but still I crawled around on my belly, reaching under the couches, calling to her. Not there.

Then I started to worry. I tried not to blame my mother for losing my rat. I couldn't bear the thought of going to sleep not knowing where Iris was, wondering if she was okay. It was getting late.

Then I had to pee. As I sat on the toilet, head in my hands, wondering what I would do if Iris had gotten lost or hurt, something caught my eye. From underneath the door of the linen closet I saw the unmistakable, beautiful sight of my baby's tail.

I opened the door and she gazed at me with a "what took you so long?" look and scampered up my legs. I smothered her with kisses.

"Why did you lock my baby in the closet?" I said as I brought her into the living room.

"Oh, thank goodness," Mom said.

"Huh," George said. "She must have gone in there and I closed the door on her."

My mother said, "Come here, you naughty girl." Instead of pointing out that nothing Iris had done was naughty except being so small as to avoid notice, I handed my rat to her grandma, who took her, kissed her on the head, and let out a big sigh of relief.

Because Ithaca is home to Cornell University, which has a premier vet school, I decided I would have Iris spayed that summer. I had read enough to know rats are prone to mammary tumors and spaying may reduce the risk.

I called the vet school, made the appointment, and brought her in. The staff, mostly young women with long ponytails, reassured me and greeted Iris with oohs and ahhs. I dropped her off and went home to wait with my ailing mother until I could pick her up.

When I went to pick up Iris the vets said she'd gone through the surgery fine, but she really didn't like having stitches. She'd tried to get them out. They made a point of telling me that as frustrated as she was, especially when they tried to keep her away from the incision, Iris never got angry, never bit anyone. "She's so gentle," these young women cooed.

To stop her from tearing out her stitches and opening her wound, they made her an Elizabethan collar, known to many dog owners as the Cone of Shame. Iris's collar was a tiny bit of white plastic that fit around her neck to keep her from messing with her belly. Unfortunately, rats don't really have necks. So she kept slipping it off.

My mother, sick and in pain, came to the rescue and distracted Iris by holding her, talking to her, telling her how brave she was and what a good patient she had been. The two of them, recovering, kept each other company, snoozing together in a sunny spot on the couch.

Iris healed quickly, though her fur, shaved for the operation, took a while to grow back. Every time I saw the bald spot I felt sick, the kind of sick you feel when you see a reminder that someone you love has been in pain.

Iris and I spent a mostly enjoyable summer in Ithaca. There were occasional squabbles—not between me and Iris; we never disagreed—because sometimes my mom forgot I was a grown-up, and sometimes I forgot to act like one.

I'd drive my mother to doctors' appointments and keep her company while she had kidney dialysis. I took it as a personal challenge to try to figure out what she might enjoy eating. Frozen macaroni-and-cheese dinners and ice-cream sandwiches proved a hit. There were lots of misses. I felt like I could never get it exactly right, and nothing I did could ease my mother's constant pain.

We did spend many hours—my mother, Iris, and I— binge-watching *Gilmore Girls* and any movie with Judi Dench in it. My mom would lie on one couch, I'd stretch out on the other, and Iris would shuttle between us.

On Sunday nights we'd have our traditional dinner: George would prepare each of us a gigantic bowl of popcorn treated with an undeniably healthy and unpredictably delicious combination of butter, olive oil, flaxseed oil, sea salt, and brewer's yeast. Iris would perch on the edge of my bowl and sift through the kernels, discarding those she deemed lacking to find one with the perfect amount of seasoning, which she would take away to a corner to eat. Then she'd come bounding back for another. When she was full, she continued the process and stashed pieces of popcorn somewhere in my mother's house. You can imagine how that went over. I had to go on search-and-destroy missions for Iris's weapons of mass mess.

During these dinners my mom would say, "Don't let her touch all of your food. That's disgusting."

And then I'd go to the bathroom during a commercial and come back to find Iris perched on the edge of my mother's popcorn bowl, sorting through her kernels.

At the end of the summer I drove back across the country to Spokane, Washington, to start my new job as a professor of creative writing.

I rented a small house in a nice residential neighborhood. My mother had been insistent I live in a house and not an apartment. When I asked why, she said because I talked to Iris all the time and if the walls were thin, I would drive someone nuts.

I said, "I don't talk to Iris all the time."

She said, "Yes, you do."

I said, "Do not."

She said, "Do too."

At that point, my mom may have stuck her tongue out at me but since we were on the phone, I couldn't see it. Then I started paying attention and realized she was right. I talked to that rat constantly.

After the summer, when I was settled in on the other side of the country and spoke to my mother on the phone, she would always ask first about her grandrat.

"Has she done anything naughty?"

I don't believe I'd ever heard my mother use the word *naughty* before that night Iris went AWOL.

"She doesn't do naughty things," I'd argue.

But still my mom would want to know what "mischief" Iris was up to.

So I told her about things I thought were adorable but that my mother might have found naughty, like when Iris went into the bathroom, reached high to get the end of the toilet paper roll, and then pulled a streamer of tissue out of the bathroom, through the hall, into my room, and onto the bed.

"Oh, that naughty girl," my mother said, and I could hear the delight in her voice.

I kept trotting out Iris stories, hoping to keep my mother

entertained and distracted. I told her how Iris had made a giant collection of things—hair ties, bits of food, a crumpled dollar bill, a pen cap—and stashed it in one of my shoes. When I went to put that shoe on I got a big surprise.

I reported on what happened when I went over to my friend Natalie's house with some big juicy steaks for her family. Natalie had gone to culinary school. I could purchase, but not cook, food. We made a good pair. I brought Iris along and she perched on my shoulder, as usual. Then, just as I went to cut off a bite of rare New York strip, she climbed down my chest, grabbed a corner of the steak, and tried to make off with it. The steak was bigger than the rat, so she didn't get far. We all had a good laugh. "Oh, that girl!" my mom said with glee when I told her about her grandrat's dinner manners.

Iris's intentions were never mischievous. She always had good reasons for her actions (nest building, planning ahead for lean times, knowing that few things taste better than a perfectly cooked steak). But my mom liked to think of her as a zany character leading an adventure-filled life. Given the increasingly limited scope of my mother's existence, I indulged her with as many stories as I could and wished I had the resourcefulness to make stuff up.

~~~~

Once, my mom called to say she'd found tiny holes in her sheets and pillowcases. I started to apologize, knowing how my mother liked her things to be "just so," explaining that Iris sometimes nibbled when she snuggled in, but my mother stopped me.

She said, "I love those holes. They remind me of my grandrat. My healer."

My mother called Iris her "healer."

A photograph that makes my heart sing

Empathy

Do animals have emotions?

Did Iris know my mother was sick?

Do animals have emotions?

When I was a kid, whenever I gave voice to something I knew one of my pets was feeling my father would laugh and say, "Don't you think you're anthropomorphizing?"

I was taught first by my father and later in school that projecting human emotions onto animals was a cardinal sin of the scientific mind. Scientists are trained to stick to measurable phenomena. Behaviors can be observed, categorized, and recorded. Feelings are more subjective and harder to pin down. At least that's the old-school way of seeing it.

Then I started reading about the research of a guy who discovered that if you tickled rats, they laughed. That interested me. What kind of person, I wondered, would spend his time tickling rats? Other than me, of course. Since the scientist was an easy hour-and-a-half drive from my home, I decided to go see him.

When I met Jaak Panksepp, the Baily Endowed Chair of Animal Well-Being Science for the Department of Veterinary and Comparative Anatomy, Pharmacology, and Physiology at Washington State University's College of Veterinary Medicine, and Emeritus Professor of the Department of Psychology at Bowling Green State University—got all that?—I told him my response to his life's work was "Duh."

He twinkled and said, "You've obviously lived with rats."

In 2003, Jaak Panksepp and Jeffrey Burgdorf published a paper called "Laughing Rats and the Evolutionary Antecedents of Human Joy?" The authors described their experiment: "After we had studied play- and reward-induced 50-kHz chirping for about three years, it occurred to us that this response might reflect some type of a 'laughter' response. During the spring of 1997, the senior author (Jaak) came to the lab, and suggested to the junior author (Jeffrey), 'Let's go tickle some rats.'"

They tickled rats—lots of rats. They tickled young rats and old rats. They tickled rats in the light and they tickled rats in the dark and found that, as anyone who has ever worked in a fluorescent-lit office can tell you, bright light suppresses laughter. They tickled rats when they were hungry. Hungrier rats laughed more (which might lead one to believe in their moral superiority to humans; we tend to get cranky when we need to eat). They tickled rats after they had handled cat hair. Not funny. They wrote, "Clearly young rats do not regard the smell of a predator as anything to chirp about." Gentle touch produced only gentle laughter; rough-and-tumble play and vigorous belly tickling produced vigorous chirping.

We're not talking here about Santa laughs or a girly *tee-hee-hee*. When rats are annoyed or anxious, they emit chirps that start at the upper range of human hearing, so occasionally a vexed and troubled rat can be heard to squeak. But like high-frequency dog whistles, much of rat communication is silent to us; beyond what we can apprehend, there's a sensory world that scientific instruments are able to translate.

Once Jaak and Jeffrey set up the equipment necessary to listen to the rats, they found that the more the humans tickled, the more the rats giggled. Young rats laugh more than older rats. When rats become accustomed to tickling, they will chirp in anticipation—the way babies, if you wiggle a finger at them and make *coochie-coo* noises, will begin to laugh before you even touch them.

Getting tickled is so much fun, rats will seek it out. Jaak and Jeffrey designed an experiment where one person petted the rats and another tickled them. When given a choice, the rats would run to the tickler. Jaak is quoted as saying, "Like a cat, or especially a dog, they stay close to you, and they follow you around—you have them chasing your hand like a pied piper."

During more than a thousand tickling sessions, no animal got pissed off. No rat ever bit a tickler with intention to harm. The most rambunctious rats, those who got superexcited, would sometimes offer a play bite. These were not threatening or painful—they were simply an expression of exuberance. The authors concluded, "Although we would be surprised if rats had a sense of humor, they certainly do appear to have a sense of fun."

Ha-ha, right? If you look on the comments of blogs and websites that feature this research, you will find people asking, in the angry tones employed by those who post vicious remarks anonymously: "Who is funding this 'science'?"

The best academic research needs to pass the "So what?" test. It has to matter in some way, whether by nudging the boundaries of a field of study, changing paradigms of the way we look at things, or bringing to light important new knowledge. It may not have ready applications, but it has to do something more than fill in postholes. Too much of what is published doesn't pass this test. But tickling rats? That matters. Let me try to explain why.

The ideas behind Jaak Panksepp's rat-tickling experiments are big. They raise questions like: Why does depression hurt? What is the importance of play? How does brain chemistry affect behavior? What are the evolutionary reasons and processes that inform our understanding of emotion? Panksepp's work combines psychology and biology to create a whole field of study, affective neuroscience, which can help us understand not only animals but also ourselves. If someone thinks it's silly to tickle rats, that person hasn't quite grasped the implications of what it means.

Not so long ago people a little different from the rest of us were treated as less than human. A good friend of mine had an autistic older brother. Her mother had been told she was a "refrigerator mother," a term used to describe women whose lack of maternal warmth caused their babies to become autistic. In other words, women got blamed for their children's brain chemistry. And these children, who didn't display "normal" emotions, were, like my friend's brother, shipped off to live in institutions.

The literary neurologist Oliver Sacks—a doctor and a writer—profiled a woman named Temple Grandin for the *New Yorker* magazine. He called the essay "An Anthropologist on Mars," the title a quote from autistic Temple about how she feels much of the time when dealing with "neuro-typical" humans—in other words, regular people. When Temple was a girl, her mother hired a nanny to work with her and she was able, though not without suffering a lot of teasing, to get through school and go to college. (If this sounds familiar, it may be because Claire Danes recently starred in a movie about her called, big surprise, *Temple Grandin*.)

Temple earned a PhD in animal science and now has a faculty position at Colorado State University. As an autistic person, she believes that her thinking and emotional responses are more similar to animals' than to other people's. Things that bother her also bother cows, but it's usually stuff ranchers never notice. For example, Temple's exquisite sensitivity to sound causes her to hear the way chains rattle. She understands that sometimes shadows look like holes in the ground. She uses her insight to help explain what it's like to be an animal and writes in strong declarative statements rare in academic work ("Cows hate yellow"; "white animals are crazy"). Academics tend to hedge and qualify and suggest and wonder instead of coming out and saying exactly what they believe. This means it's easier and more fun to read writing by Temple than by most other scientists. She has long been a consultant to the meat industry and invented a process used to comfort frightened cattle en route to slaughter.

Temple Grandin draws heavily on Jaak Panksepp's work to make her arguments. She references core emotions as a way of understanding how animals feel the things they feel. Temple's contributions to the field are primarily in the real-world applications of Jaak's ideas. She has been responsible for many changes that make the process of producing meat more humane because she understands how cows feel.

At this point in history, it's hard for some of us to remember that not all people accept evolutionary theory. But it's even more challenging for me to realize many of the most staunch supporters of Darwin and his legacy still don't believe that animals—our scientific test models for pretty much every drug used in humans—are similar to us in having emotions. Perhaps these doubting scientists need some sessions tickling rats.

Marc Bekoff is perhaps the best-known scientist of animal emotions. He is Emeritus Professor of Ecology and Evolutionary Biology at the University of Colorado, Boulder, which makes him sound august and, well, aged. But he bikes about a zillion miles and seems to have more energy than many teenagers. With the famed primatologist Jane Goodall, he co-founded Ethologists for the Ethical Treatment of Animals: Citizens for Responsible Animal Behavior Studies. *Ethologist* is a fancy name for a person who studies animal behavior. I didn't learn this until I was in my thirties and started hanging out with ethologists.

Bekoff has published more than twenty books, many for a popular readership. He writes a lot about animal emotion and provides the intellectual framework for much of the work of animal protectionists—those who believe we need to use animals in science, but we must set ethical parameters to decide what's okay to do to them. Bekoff writes, "It's bad biology to argue against the existence of animal emotions. Scientific research in evolutionary biology, cognitive ethology, and social neuroscience supports the view that numerous and diverse animals have rich and deep emotional lives. Emotions have evolved as adaptations in numerous species, and they serve as a social glue to bond animals with one another."

In December 2011, on his Huffington Post blog, Bekoff wrote, "Anyone who's kept up with the latest and greatest about the cognitive, emotional, and moral lives of nonhuman animals ('animals') knows 'surprises' are being uncovered almost daily and many non-primate animals are showing intellectual and emotional capacities that rival those of the great apes." One such surprise was work written up in an article in *Science* by University of Chicago researchers about empathy in rats.

When I saw Peggy Mason on TV, in a *NOVA* episode, I guessed I would like her. When I met her, it took about seven seconds for me to realize I was correct. A few years ago I made a trip to the South Side of Chicago and met with Peggy and her collaborator, Inbal Ben-Ami Bartal. Designed by Inbal, then a graduate student who had been doing work on empathy in humans and wanted to find a biological basis for it, the experiment worked like this: They put two cage-mates together in an arena, but one of them was placed in a restraining tube. The free-range rat could roam around, but the other was imprisoned. The researchers observed that the free rat would become agitated when another rat was stuck in the tube. After several days, the free rat would learn how to open the tube door and liberate her companion. The drive toward freeing the other trumped even the appeal of a pile of chocolate chips; the free rat would release her companion before chowing down.

Peggy is quoted in the *New York Times* as saying, "They then did what we refer to as a celebration. The trapped rat runs around the arena, and the free rat appears excited and runs after the trapped rat." Perhaps not surprising to some of us, female rats tended to be door openers. Mason says, "The females, once they open the door, they open the door every day, and within a few minutes. But the male rats would occasionally take off a day."

The initial experiment got a lot of attention. Rats feel empathy! That was big news. Even the haters found the research fascinating. But the next round of questions the scientists asked might be even more interesting and have bigger repercussions.

In another paper Peggy and Inbal discussed their discovery that rats were more likely to help other rats if they were familiar with their type. Albino rats consistently freed other albino rats, even if they'd never met before. But when black-hooded rats were trapped, the albinos didn't free them—unless, and here's the kicker, the albino had been raised with the hooded rats. To see if they would open the door for a stranger who looked different, the researchers had an albino live with a hooded rat for two weeks, and then go back to having an albino cage-mate. Then they tested the albino to see if she'd open the door for a hooded stranger. She would.

"Rats are apparently able to categorize others into groups and modify their social behavior according to group membership," Inbal wrote. "Genetic similarity or relatedness to another individual really has no influence at all."

So all that teaching about diversity? The drive to integrate schools so kids are exposed to people who look different from them? It's a good idea and may pay off to make us better citizens of the world.

Start paying attention to scientific news and you'll see more and more mind-blowing studies on animal emotion.

Take the work of Anne Hanson, a scientist and rat owner herself. After graduating from Stanford, Anne went to the University of California at Davis to get a PhD in animal behavior. At the time, she had three pet rats: Cricket, Widget, and Snip. As a rat person, she loved them. As a scientist, she observed their behavior, searched the literature for answers, and performed experiments.

She also participated on a busy pet-rat-owners listserv with thousands of members. Eventually she created her own website, www.ratbehavior.org. She remembers, "Rat owners would ask questions about their rats' behavior, and I would research answers, write them up from the perspective of a professional behavioral biologist, and post them to the list. These were very well received, and after a while I realized I should collect these answers and post them somewhere so they wouldn't be lost. That was the nucleus of the website."

Then, because scientists tend to be curious and

inquisitive—a lot, in fact, like rats—she became fascinated with the topic and the site grew ever more complex. "My goal was to bring the scientific literature on rats to the public in a way that would be more accessible than a journal article."

This is no small task. Much of what is published in scholarly journal articles is painful for people like you and me to read. Scientists are trained to think in a particular fashion, but they don't always learn to communicate what they've discovered in ways that are intelligible to others. They absorb a lot of jargon—language specific to their discipline and not understood by those outside of it. They tend to use long words that don't conjure a specific image. Or, to put that previous sentence another way, a way that a scientist might write, "The tendency is to utilize polysyllabic linguistic abstractions." Which line would you rather read?

Anne Hanson did all of us a big favor when she waded through thousands of pages that are difficult for a layperson to understand and translated them into clear prose. During the course of her reading, she made a discovery. She says,

> I realized, during my years of working on this, that
> the vast majority of scientific articles written about
> rats are not about understanding the rats for

themselves. They are about using the rats as a model for other systems, usually the human system. Rats, in these articles, are almost completely divorced from their evolutionary and ecological context—they are simply furry test tubes, not rodents from northern China that became commensal with humans thousands of years ago and have a fascinating evolutionary history and behavioral repertoire of their own.

Anne slips in one word here that marks her as a specialist: *commensal.* She uses it because it's exactly the word she means. *Commensalism* is "a relation between two kinds of organisms in which one obtains food or other benefits from the other without damaging or benefiting it." In other words, she found scientists weren't looking at rats as subjects of their own rat lives, only as tagalongs to people. She explains to me,

> Of the small minority of articles that examined rat behavior for its own sake, most of those did so in the lab and still had little connection with the rats' natural context. Only a tiny minority of articles examined rat behavior in a wild or semi-wild context. So a second goal of mine became to hunt

down the few articles that looked at natural rat behavior, and bring those to light on my website.

Anne discovered holes in the ethological literature when it came to the behavior of rats. She got interested in what was missing. One of the field's founders, Niko Tinbergen, who wanted to make an objective science of the study of animal behavior, invented a tool called an "ethogram," a catalog of behaviors for each species. Anne couldn't find one for rats, so she put together an informal one herself.

As a student, she looked to apply the things she learned about other species to her beloved rats. She put forth hypotheses about them, some of which were later proven correct.

At a time when most students are tortured by the writing they have to do to produce a dissertation—spending hours in libraries and laboratories and crafting painful reports of their own research—Anne used her website as a creative outlet. She could work on what she wanted to as a warm-up for the harder stuff. She got to write fun, interesting entries rather than dry academic prose.

After earning her PhD, Anne got a job as a field biologist and project director at a bird observatory, and then left to start a family. Currently she's at home with three young children. She no longer has pet rats, but hopes to have them again someday.

The work Anne put into her exhaustive, scientific, and fun-to-read website paid off professionally as well: another scientist asked her to collaborate on a chapter on rats for a veterinary textbook. You never know what will happen when you write only to please yourself; if you're passionate about the subject and take care to do it well, you might be surprised at the success that follows.

Anne, with the ardor of all of us rat lovers but with a scientist's knowledge and insight, pointed out to me reasons why rats might make better pets than other small critters. We are always looking for reasons to defend our love, and she has some good ones. For example, she notes that rats are social in the wild, and this translates to sociability as pets (unlike hamsters, who are solitary in the wild, and therefore solitary in captivity).

Anne says,

A tame rat likes being around people, hanging out with people, being petted, and playing with you. Rats are versatile and adaptable in the wild, and this makes them easy to train in the pet context. Rats are also larger than many other rodent pets, which makes them a bit more confident around people and easier to handle (rats are about the size of a human hand, which makes them easier to hold, when compared to, say, mice) but they're also agile climbers, which makes them okay with being picked up.

She compares them to guinea pigs, who are nonclimbing ground dwellers and don't like being hoisted in the air.

Since rats have been domesticated for a long time, Anne notes that "the domestic trait of calmness around humans has had longer to stabilize (unlike hamsters, which have only been domesticated for forty to fifty years, or dwarf hamsters, which were domesticated even more recently)." If you've ever held a dwarf hamster, you know what she's talking about.

"I've heard rats described as the 'poor man's dog' and find the comparison very apt," Anne says. "They're small, social, easy to train, and cheap."

After doing research into the neuroscience of emotion, after learning about the experiments on empathy, after reading a lot of the ethological literature on rat behavior, I felt I had an answer to my question.

Yes. I believe that Iris did know my mother was sick. Not only do I believe Iris knew, I think she wanted to do everything she could to make my mother feel better, even if she couldn't heal her.

Fern (top) and Laurel in their sleeping hut

The Rescuer
What kind of person has forty-three rats?

Iris and I settled into our new home in Spokane.

I put her cage in the second bedroom I used as an office and propped it off the floor to avoid drafts. I created another set of steps out of books leading to the door so when I opened it she could come and go as she pleased. I put her travel cage in a corner of the living room as a litter box. She liked to pee and poop in there.

We adapted our routines to the new space. Mornings I'd get up early to open her door, we'd go to our separate places to pee, and then we'd meet in my bed and snuggle for a couple more hours before I went to work. I invited my colleagues and students to come over because Iris loved visitors. During a birthday party for a friend, Iris leaped onto the coffee table and tried to make off with an entire cupcake. A naughty story for my mother! The house had a fireplace I never used that Iris loved to explore, often emerging looking more dirty than the pre-ball Cinderella.

One night we were playing Flying Squirrel. If you're not familiar with this superfun game, here's how it works: Iris would stand on her hind legs, hook her armpits over my fingers, and gaze at me. I would zoom her around, letting her stretch her back. Sometimes I'd hang her above my mouth and kiss her big pink feet. But on this night, as I held her face in front of mine, I saw she had a lump on her cheek.

A lump.

She'd been spayed at Cornell that summer precisely to stave off the possibility of tumors. Was this a tumor? How could she have a tumor? She was only nine months old.

I went to the Internet to find a vet in my new hometown and nabbed an appointment at seven the next morning. I didn't sleep that night.

Keri was like many vets: an articulate, attractive woman who clearly loved animals. But she looked young. I knew enough doctors to know that medicine is as much an art as it is a science. A lot of treatment has to do with a physician's ability to develop a good gut—a feeling for disease. You get this by seeing many cases. I worried this nice young woman hadn't been out of school long enough, or treated enough rats (admittedly not the most popular pets), for me to trust her with my baby.

So I asked. Without getting defensive when a semihysterical rat mother quizzed her on her experience, Keri told me she saw lots of rats, often the pets of the elderly or infirm. They were, she said, easy to care for and, as we know, loving and responsive and clever and wonderful. Plus, she said, one of her clients had forty-five rats, so just working with that woman, she'd seen a lot of different problems.

Reassured, I left Iris with her and went home. Keri called within an hour to say she had lanced an abscess and put in a couple of stitches; she said Iris was still woozy from the anesthesia, but I could come and pick up my sweet girl. She called her a sweet girl. I fell a little in love with Keri then and was sorry I'd demanded to know her credentials.

Driving back to the clinic, I thought about the Rat Lady, the woman who kept forty-five rats and brought them in— spending considerable amounts of time and money—to have them spayed, detumored, and treated. I formed a picture of what such a person would look like, imagined her life, and thought I'd like to meet her because she was probably interesting, though in a sad, freaky kind of way. One rat is often considered odd; forty-five seems pathological, even to me.

Standing by the front desk when I arrived at the vet office was a young, well-dressed couple. On the counter rested a cage lined with soft, fleecy blankets, containing four rats. One, an albino, was sleeping, stretched out. Another poked around in the blankets. A third stood on top of the albino's head. And the last kept trying to climb out of the cage.

The guy wore a black leather jacket, had fashionable facial hair, and cooed gently at the rats. The woman—beautiful, late twenties, long dark hair, big dark eyes, a ready smile— told me, when I asked, that these girls were going to be spayed today. We had a couple of exchanges and then it hit me: "Are you the woman with forty-five rats?"

She gave a sad smile and a correction. "Forty-three now."

Her name, she said, was Tori and we chatted for a while. I told her about Iris, told her I was interested in rats. She invited me to come and see hers and we made plans.

I followed her directions as I drove north of Spokane, past wheat fields, and over a pass to Loon Lake. They had a motor home and a boat in the front yard of a big house, and a BMW SUV in the driveway. Tori invited me in, and we went downstairs. The basement floor was covered by a brindled shag carpet and we had to step over a barrier—a board meant to block unsanctioned adventures—into a room with a huge TV and a comfortably overstuffed sectional sofa. Here, Tori said, Dave watched television and played with the rats.

We entered another big room. Along the walls gigantic black metal cages, each with three stories, made me feel immediately inadequate, given the size of Iris's. Each had an uppermost story with brightly colored hammocks made of fleece; below were wooden huts. Some cages had extra cardboard boxes; some had running wheels. When we entered, no one was awake.

Tori had clearly given the tour before. We started with a cage that housed the rats I'd met at the vet's office, a blended family of mostly young girls. They'd come back from their surgeries—spaying—looking fit and fine. Next to them was the geriatric cage. Here lived old ladies, grizzled, slow, all nearly three years old, though Tori recorded their ages in a lined notebook in months. Among them was Dizzy.

Tori and the vet believed Dizzy had a pituitary tumor because she had started rolling around, but she was too old to operate on. When she walked she twitched and wobbled, but otherwise seemed content. Elderly Betty, Tori told me, had been left at the door of a nearby Petco.

Somehow, once word of the fact that Tori rescued rats got out, she became the one to call. This is how you can end up with more than forty rats.

The diabetic cage had obese rats who, Tori told me, were the only ones who might ever bite. At first she thought they were just mean, ill-tempered. But then they were diagnosed and she had been working to control their blood sugar with diet. The eight diabetics, corpulent biters, were huge. Normally, female rats weigh 12 to 14 ounces. Roadie weighed in at 28.5 ounces. "She's lost an ounce and a half," said proud Tori.

Tori took Roadie out and put her on the floor. She looked like a mop with a tiny pointy head. Her flab covered her legs and it amazed me she could walk. But she could.

Dave bounded around dispensing uncooked noodles. As the rats ate, the room started to sound like car wheels on a gravel road from the noise of the crunching. He stopped at the diabetic cage.

"Don't you dare," said Tori.

"Oh, please."

"No."

"A little piece?"

She wagged a finger and shot him a look.

"There's broccoli upstairs," she said. "You can give them that." As he trotted out of the room she called after him, "Don't forget to wash it."

Ray had no eyes. He was born that way. "We keep thinking he really can see, because he gets around so well," said Tori.

"He's the most adventurous of all the rats," chimed in Dave, back from the kitchen with a handful of food.

Twiggy came from the same litter as the diabetics. Twiggy, a hairless rat, looked to me like an anteater, with pink skin and rolls of fat. "We called him Twiggy because his tail is messed up," said Tori as she pointed out an appendage that segmented into inch-and-a-half sections that went off in different directions, like, you guessed it, a twig.

The Nilla cage was like Plymouth Rock, the initial settlement of the colony, where the first descendants of the first arrivals lived. Their grandmother had been the first female, and she was pregnant when Dave and Tori took her in. When Tori introduced me to the rats in the Nilla cage, I got to hear the story of how this couple came to have such an abundance of rats.

At the time Tori and Dave met, he was a snake guy. He owned two red-tailed boas and two ball pythons. You can guess what he fed them. But one day, his snakes refused dinner, which turned out to be Ratigan. Dave had always liked the rats.

"It got harder and harder; I used to watch them and be fascinated," he said.

Dave came home one day to the sounds of screaming. Tori had a snake in one hand and a dead rat in the other. She was crying. They brought the snake back to the store.

"The guy said he couldn't give me any money for it. I told him I didn't care. I just didn't want it anymore."

Not long after that, they began adopting rats.

We moved on to the Creamy cage, which was filled with blond rats and many more toys than in the other cages. These guys, Tori said, were the thinkers and the doers. If they got bored, they would chew through their plastic dog bowls or bite into the water bottle hung on the outside of their cage. These were the super-high achievers, the Advanced Placement kids. Like many of us who breezed through honors classes, they were not without their tics and quirks.

For example, Azi was a "barber." When her active mind didn't have enough to do, she would groom herself mercilessly, eventually losing hair and causing sores. Sonny was a Dumbo. Sonny's huge round ears, set farther back on his head, made him look like a Disneyfied version of a rat, the way Mickey went from pointy to round. Sonny was irresistible, perhaps not just because of the roundness we associate with cute, but because he bumbled around.

"It's a community," said Tori. "They all have different personalities—they're so different. Azi is like the smart cheerleader. Sonny, he's the chubby sweet boy."

Sonny was like a Walmart greeter. Tori took him out of the cage and, as soon as we sat on the floor, he came waddling over. Tori explained that they let the rats out on a schedule; each group got time to play. When they had their fill of exploring, they "put themselves away," Tori said. Stairs led to the door of each cage, and the rats decided when it was time to go home.

Sonny, I must say, turned out to be a loving chunk of rat. He crawled over me, onto my hand, wanting to be near. Azi was more standoffish. I realized neither of them was like Iris, who was more people oriented and outgoing. As much as I enjoyed meeting these rats, I realized how individual they were. Their personalities were so pronounced, the rats so easily distinguishable, it was hard to imagine anyone confusing them.

We moved on to the cage of Pretty Boys, which included Charlie, the bad rat, and Jojo and Bobo, both blond and fat. Jojo was one of the few who preferred Tori to Dave. Tori's role was that of the disciplinarian, the giver of nasty-tasting medicines and shots, the person who checked them over and kept them healthy. Dave cuddled them and gave them treats. He cooed. He gushed.

"Whenever we get a new rat," Tori said, "Dave will hold him tight for an hour or so. At first the rat will squirm and try to get away. And then he settles down. And later, when they're out to play, they come over to Dave and they'll cuddle up with him while he's sleeping or watching TV." She said this with the resignation of a mother content to do the caring, not minding being the less fun of the pair.

I watched as Dave handled each rat. When he picked one up, he cradled him in his hands, holding him on his back. None of the rats struggled. They just lay there, relaxed and calm and trusting.

In the final cage I met the descendants of Freya. "It's a bad line," Tori said. "This family tends to develop tumors. Four of the six girls have died, leaving Maisy and Winnie." Tori bought two albino rats because she wanted them. Part of the reason Tori got all her rats spayed is because they are so prone to mammary tumors.

Tori read the medical literature exhaustively. She cared for more sick rats than many small animal vets. Each morning Tori and Dave did a cage check, going through and looking over the rats to make sure everyone was okay. They had gotten up to fifty-six, but a population of forty-three was more manageable. "Thirteen rats makes a big difference," Tori said.

She prepared their food, her own special blend of a variety of organic cereals. "I like Kashi a lot because it's low sodium," she said. She included Puffins "for their sweet tooth," Pirate's Booty made of spinach and kale, maple-flavored buckwheat flakes, and dog food—the natural kind, used for weight management in older dogs. "It has glucosamine and chondroitin," Tori said. She used Care-FRESH litter, the same bedding I used for my one small rat. "They all seem to pee at the bottom of their stairs," she said. That's exactly where Iris liked to pee.

When I asked Tori about health issues she said, "We've had to learn the hard way." Once, they stepped on a rat. "We didn't know that she was just in shock and that what we needed was to wrap her in warm blankets. We brought her to the vet and he put her in a tank that chilled her and she died."

She showed me a medicine chest's worth of hospital gear: syringes, glue for incisions and little cuts, gauze, and "ratty morphine." This is what they would have given Iris, she told me, for pain management after her abscess surgery.

"How do you know when a rat is in pain?" I asked, knowing how stoic my baby was.

"Their hair stands up. They hunch. They won't leave you alone," Tori explained. "They want to be up in your face, on your neck."

Iris liked to hang out on my neck and I started worrying

maybe I'd been missing something. Had she not been feeling well all that time? Tori said no, I would know the difference between seeking affection and needing comfort.

"Here, I'll show you the hair thing," she said, and she took out Jojo, a "soldier rat." He was aggressive. She brought him over to Azi, who was still prowling around, checking things out. He chased her for a while and then his blond hairs stuck up in a Mohawk. Like a dog or cat, he made himself look bigger. I know this is called piloerection. I'm sure I remember this word because I think it's funny.

One of the remarkable things about rats is their ethic of care: the old and sick take care of one another. Tori described Albert, an old guy. "I put Sierra, a middle-aged female, in with him. It got so he couldn't walk. Every morning when I'd come down, Sierra would have scooted the food bowl over to Albert."

I'd heard about this kind of helping behavior. Tori had seen it. She'd seen so much.

We sat on the floor of the rat room and went through her notebook. She showed me the detailed descriptions of each rat: when they were born, the medical problems they had faced, and then short obituaries. In these notes I saw the girl that she still was—unreconstructed emotion next to clinical expressions. "I will miss you," she had written beside the record of the number of months each rat had lived.

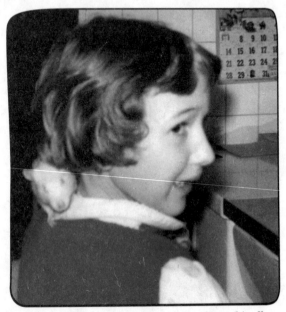

Debbie Ducommun with the rat that changed it all

The Rat Lady

Where do you go for expert advice?

When I adopted Iris I was lucky to find a veterinarian (Keri) who saw lots of rats because she had a client (Tori) who had lots of rats. When it comes to caring for "exotic" pets, it can be hard to find a vet who knows how to treat them.

I wondered: Where do you go for good information about rats?

If you look on the Internet, as we all know, you get what you pay for. It's as easy to find an "expert" as it is to step in dog poop in the park. Now you can find a gazillion Facebook groups and websites and breeders (more on that soon), but still I wondered, who really knows this stuff?

That would be the Rat Lady.

Debbie Ducommun remembers finding a metal cage under the Christmas tree one year. Actually, what she remembers is a metal cage, a furry hamster, and an ouchy bite. She does not know what happened to the hamster after that. Then she got a mouse. Then, while in grade school, since her elder sister had had a rat, she got a rat. In high school she got another one, who turned out to be pregnant. As I've mentioned before, this is not uncommon when you get a rat from a pet store. So then she had multiple rats.

Debbie's family lived in an orchard, growing prunes and almonds. They had the usual farm menagerie of dogs and cats, chickens for eggs, rabbits for meat, plus salamanders, lizards, and crawfish. There were always critters around. When she went to college she majored in animal behavior and after graduation got a job as a vet assistant. She later managed a humane society. She took a position in a psych lab at Cal State Chico in 1985 and started to be known as the Rat Lady.

"Hello, this is Debbie the Rat Lady," she says when she answers her phone these days. It rings frequently and her email in-box is always full. If you contact her at the address listed on her website, ratfanclub.org, you will get an automated reply saying she gets so much email you may not hear from her.

In her capacity as self-appointed Rat Lady in the 1980s, people brought her their rats and their rat questions. She answered them and found herself drawn to the idea of writing a book. She put together a proposal, but found no publishers interested in pet rat care. So she started the Rat Fan Club and published a newsletter to disseminate her rat knowledge. The membership grew to the low triple figures.

In 1998, she finally found a publisher for *Rats! A Fun and Care Book*, which she revised and updated once in 2002 as *Rats: Practical, Accurate Advice from the Expert* and then again in 2011. (BowTie Press, Debbie's first publisher, was the book division of pet magazines *Cat Fancy* and *Dog Fancy*. Believe it or not, there is currently no *Rat Fancy*, even though pet rats are also known as fancy rats and that would be a killer title for a magazine for rat fanciers.)

Debbie the Rat Lady is about as famous as someone can get as an expert on how to care for pet rats. That, of course, can make her a controversial figure in the small community of rat lovers. Some people love her, some disapprove of her, but no one can argue about her commitment to rats. Debbie has educated herself to be able to diagnose most rat illnesses by phone or email. She knows which drugs work, and unlike many vets who do not see big numbers of ratty patients, she claims to know when rat physiology is not analogous to that of dogs and cats. According to her website, Debbie has promoted rats on many well-known television shows. She's frequently called on as an expert by anyone who has an interest in rats.

And she gets calls from lots of rat owners.

On the day we spoke, she described her morning to me. She'd had a call from someone who worried her rat was going senile. Over the phone Debbie diagnosed a pituitary tumor. It's a common problem with older rats and the only treatment available at that time was prednisone, which would buy three to six more weeks of normal functioning before the rat would start to decline again. Three to six weeks in animals who don't last more than two and a half years is nothing to sneeze at.

Sneezing is, however, another big problem. Pet-store rats are often afflicted with respiratory ailments. "Most pet rats being sold are not good-quality animals," the Rat Lady says. "They are not genetically selected or properly socialized. They're often sick. These places are the equivalent of puppy mills. People buying from a pet store are not going to get the best experience with their first pet rat." Selective breeding is the key to having good pets, she says, something all serious rat people would agree with.

Debbie started a nonprofit organization, the Rat Assistance & Teaching Society (called, of course, by the acronym RATS), whose main goal is to help educate the pet-care industry about the proper treatment of rats. She wants the big chains to stop selling rats as live snake food. Petco does this, but PetSmart doesn't. The Rat Lady doesn't mind when people feed their snakes mice and rats, but she wants the rodents to be euthanized and then frozen first. It's more humane, she says.

"Feeder rats" is perhaps the most contentious issue in the rat community. Many people come to love rats after offering them to their snakes as dinner. Some, like Tori and Dave, give up the reptiles and switch their allegiance to the rodents; others manage to make peace with the situation and keep both, just as animal lovers like me continue to eat meat.

The Rat Lady lives in California, the state with the largest population of pet rats. The oldest club, the American Fancy Rat & Mouse Association (AFRMA), is based in Los Angeles, founded by a mother-daughter team. Why are Californians so rat-friendly? First, Debbie says, rat people tend to be rather open-minded and liberal. She also believes rats are more of a lower- and middle-class pet. "Not a lot of millionaire rat owners," she says, but then confesses she doesn't know a lot of millionaires. "They probably have dogs," she says. "Many of the rat club people are women, but that doesn't necessarily mean more women own rats; they just tend to be joiners."

Oh, and perhaps the reason so many Californians pick

rats as their exotic pets is because basically everything else is illegal. Sure, you can get your hamsters, gerbils, ferrets, and guinea pigs. But no sugar gliders, hedgehogs, primates, big cats, wild dogs, crocodiles, or elephants. This is both to keep California safe from the destructive influence of non-native intruders, and also, since it is California, to look out for the dispossessed, because wild animals should be wild.

When Pixar wanted to make *Ratatouille*, they invited Debbie Ducommun to bring a handful of her rats and talk to them about rat behavior. They filmed her rats and ended up having a rat at the studio.

Debbie knows a thing or two about training rats and in 2008 published a book called *The Complete Guide to Rat Training*. Her basic idea is that if you want a creature, human or otherwise, to do something, you have to figure out what's important to it. And what's important to one animal might not be the same thing for a different animal of the same species. You might care about money; I might be nudged along by the prospect of having you clean my house or bake me cookies. One of the points Debbie makes in the book is that in order to train your rat to do tricks, you have to know your rat as an individual and figure out what's most important to him or her. Just as you would never make a claim like "All girls love pink," you might not be able to say, "All rats love peanut butter." In fact, I used to say this a lot (based on my experiences with Hester and Iris) until I met rats who, shocking as it may seem, didn't love peanut butter.

Debbie explains what a happy rat does. A happy rat will grind her teeth. It's called "bruxing" and is like a cat purring. A superhappy rat will bug out her eyes. This, I've learned, is called "boggling," though in her book Debbie calls it "eye popping." Iris used to brux and boggle, though I never knew the words and didn't know, because my sample was so small and I hadn't read any books, if this was an Iris thing or a rat thing. A rat thing, as it turns out.

Debbie stresses positive reinforcement in training and says because rats are so curious, it's easy to take advantage of their willingness to explore when you want them to interact with a new toy or climb on or in something. She also likes "clicker training." Basically, after you ask the rat to do something and she does it—or even starts to do it—you make a clicking noise right away, so she associates this sound with doing the right thing. Then you follow up by giving her a treat. In her head the sequence is do it, hear it, eat it. For a few bucks you can buy a clicker at a pet store.

The hard part is stopping them from doing things you don't want them to do. I've always been struck by how when animals accidentally hurt you—when puppies bite, horses nip, cats claw, or my pig, Emma, would step on your stomach with her pointy hooves—and you yelp *Ouch!*, they will often back off and even look ashamed. Everyone seems to understand the language of pain.

More difficult is getting them to refrain from harming your books, shoes, and sheets. Rodents chew. There are products you can smear on surfaces that might taste bad enough to rats to keep them from gnawing. But Debbie says rats' mouths are designed "with special cheek folds that keep gnawed material from entering the mouth cavity" and "by the time the rat tastes the product, he has already taken a chunk out of the protected object."

Because I was such a helicoptering rat parent, Iris rarely got to chow down on anything without me noticing. She did sometimes go into the closet and, um, decorate some of my shoes. When she lay on my legs she tended to dreamily move her mouth in such a way that small holes appeared in my jeans. I never seemed to catch her in the act, since I was usually deep into a book. She did the same thing to sheets and pillowcases.

None of the damage was dangerous to her, so I figured she was teaching me a lesson about not getting too attached to material possessions. Or about the silliness of buying expensive Italian leather shoes.

The first thing rats need to be trained to do is to trust you. Debbie calls this "trust training," though I would probably call it something like dating.

When you first get a rat, he may be scared. He needs to get to know you—your scent, your voice, your personality. Debbie's advice on this is clear. First you put food on a spoon and put the spoon in the cage. Then you have him come to the door of the cage for the treat-laden spoon. You gradually move the spoon out into the world and expect the rat to follow. This might seem obvious, but many who are eager to be their new pet's BFF are tempted to reach in and grab. It might be helpful here to think of the dating analogy. How would you feel if a stranger grabbed you? Do you want something that's over in a flash or a long-term relationship?

Rats are fastidious about keeping clean. This makes it easy to train them to use a litter box. Debbie seems to believe more in nurture than in nature when it comes to toilet training. "I think that a rat's bathroom habits have a lot to do with the habitat in which he grew up as a baby, as well as the bathroom habits of his mother." Basically she says parenting makes a difference in the manners of the kid. Slovenly moms will reproduce themselves.

As you read her book on training, two themes become clear: you have to watch and get to know your rat, and you have to be patient. One of the advantages of having seen a lot of rats over the years is that Debbie knows how much individual difference there is. She talks about shy rats and those who are outgoing (she attributes much of this to handling early in their lives), active rats and lazy ones (usually the boys are lazy), those who pee and poop in a tidy corner and those who can't be bothered to go downstairs when nature calls. You know—they're like people. The same and really, really different.

Debbie gives instructions for teaching your rat to stand (they do this anyway—like much of training, it becomes simply a matter of giving a name to a behavior and then rewarding it), kiss (you put food on your face, she licks it off—not like dating), spinning or twirling (every animal I've ever lived with has twirled for food—dogs, cats, rats, pigs, boys). Trickier tricks take advantage of the fact that rats are incredible athletes. They can be taught things that require balance, like walking on a tightrope, climbing, and jumping from one platform to another.

I never bothered to teach Iris tricks for the sake of performing, but asked her to use all of her skills to do things like balance on my shoulder as I walked or ran, or scale the bed like a mountain climber. On her own she mastered the Olympic skill of launching herself at my leg. I'd be standing in the kitchen washing dishes and all of a sudden something would land on the back of my thigh. It would of course be Iris, who would cling to my jeans, assess the best approach, feel for handholds, like my pockets, and clamber up until she summited on my shoulder.

Most of the tricks you can train your rat to do involve the same process—letting them know what you want by rewarding them with clicks and treats—and a ton of patience.

You can hitch a tiny basket to a string, put a treat in the basket, and let your rat pull it up. Debbie says you need to show the rat where the treat is. You can teach a lazy rat to stay by rewarding him with a treat when he stays. And then you can humiliate him by balancing something on his head and rewarding him for sitting there like a dunce. You can get rats to ride on toy trucks, or push carts, or even wear a harness and pull a cart, though Iris hated her harness and would Houdini herself out of it in seconds.

Debbie says you can go to the dollar store to buy tiny props, like mini basketballs or furniture, and you can create dazzling displays. If you do this, please take lots of photos and send them to me.

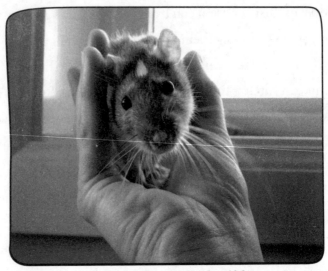

As a baby, Iris could be a handful

The Secret Society

Who are the rat lovers?

I was lucky to meet Tori at the vet's office, and I found Debbie because I'm a book person. But who else loved rats as much as I did? Where do the rat people hang out?

When I first moved to Durham, North Carolina, from Manhattan, my circle of friends came from the dog club. It wasn't actually a club, just a portion of the Duke campus where each day after work a bunch of people congregated so their dogs could play together. You formed friendships without ever knowing one another's names beyond Hannah's mom or Moe's dad, standing around in clumps chatting while your dogs sniffed one another's butts and chased balls.

There was no equivalent informal rat club. And it's not like people announce their ratly love by wearing sweaters with images of their beloved pets (though some do) or join playgroups. There are plenty of boutique pet stores where you can bump into other folks willing to spend gobs of dough on their nonhuman companions, but dogs and cats have cornered the pet merchandise market. No one stands in front of the rat food, starts talking to strangers as they pick up bags of pellets, and says, "Hey, let's get our little darlings together."

My students knew about Iris because, well, I talked about her all the time. She was a great icebreaker, a way for me to let students into my world and get to know me as a person, not just a teacher.

We choose our pets the way we choose everything else. Sometimes practical considerations hold sway. If you live in a small apartment, your best bet is probably not a Great Dane. If you don't like to go outside and get dirty, you're not going to be a horse person. Also, if you don't have buckets of money, you should probably stay away from the equine world.

Sometimes we're carried by impulse and by our own predilections. I have too many shoes that look similar (black with chunky heels) because I see a pair in a store and think,

I have to have these. What I don't think is, *I already have fourteen pairs exactly like this.*

Sometimes we fall into things. Someone says, "Hey, wanna come for a run?" Instead of saying, "No, I don't run. In fact, I'd rather pound my own head with a mallet," you say, "Okay. I'll try it." You never planned to be a runner, and even twenty years and sixty or so marathons later you think, *I'm a runner? How did that happen?*

And sometimes we make choices as reflections of ourselves, of both who we think we are and who we want to be. Often when people go shopping for a new house they see a formal dining room and imagine themselves having elaborate dinner parties, even though they hate to cook and don't like hosting. They ignore everything about how they actually live and escape into a fantasy of what life would be like, if only.

Rat people know that when we take our darlings out in public, we announce ourselves to the world. Aligning oneself with rats, a maligned, misunderstood, and reviled group, can seem empowering, like flipping a rebellious middle finger to the world.

Once, a friend and I went into one of those pet superstores so I could get some food for Iris. We stopped, of course, to peer at the rodents on display. I will confess to an all-too-human delight in looking at hamsters because, even though I know they're nippy little jerks, they are cute as all get-out. As we stood gazing at the roly-poly sociopaths, a family came lumbering into the store.

These three huge people looked like they'd ridden in on motorcycles. They dressed in leather, stained denim, and boots reinforced with metal, and had tattoos like the type people had before everyone had tattoos. The big man wore a baseball cap sideways and a heavy-metal shirt. The woman's generous flesh filled out her less-than-generous clothes. The kid that accompanied them could only have been their progeny.

Hitching a ride on the shoulders of each of the grown-ups was a big rat. These two also looked like members of the family. Substantial, they were. Solid.

We had to speak with them. We asked about the rats and they started talking and didn't stop. They loved their rats— the best pets, they said. They told us stories and I brought Iris into the conversation *(I'm like you! I understand!)* and we compared notes and behaviors. This family charmed us with their gentleness and made us think hard about the assumptions we'd made on first seeing them. They'd had rats for a long time.

The best pets, they said again.

~~~~

On the other hand, my college roommate Val is about the last person on earth you would suspect of being a rat lover. Val had spent some time with Iris, but not a lot. She had never been much of an animal person. Once I took her horseback riding, and, let's just say, it didn't go that well. When I introduced her to my friend Sal the Llama, and Sal stuck his face right into hers, Val said in a calm and measured voice, "Rach, I'm not liking this," and backed away.

If you met Val, in her interestingly textured clothes and sculpted haircut, if you learned about her fancy job giving away millions of dollars for one of America's biggest foundations and talked to her for the three minutes it takes to realize how smart and worldly and sophisticated she is, you might not guess she's a rat person. (Unless, of course, you are a true rat person and recognize what a diverse group we are.)

For Val it started when her daughter, Ivy, volunteered to keep one of the classroom pets over spring break.

Ivy was, at the time, six years old. She knew which animal she wanted and worried someone would call dibs before she did. But even if she had chosen last, she still wouldn't have had competition. No one else wanted to take Lemon home.

Ivy knew she could take good care of Lemon. She liked rats. She'd met a good rat (Iris), and she could always ask me, her Auntie Rachel, if she had questions. Val phoned before they brought Lemon home to say I'd be on call during Lemon's visit. Fine with me.

I gave Val some pointers—let Lemon run around on the bed; broccoli is like crack to rats; expect some peeing outside of the cage but no pooping—and looked forward to hearing how things went.

When spring break ended, Val called.

"Well," she said, drawing the word out to about four beats, "it was interesting."

She told me Ivy had done great with Lemon. Ivy taught her mother how to let Lemon out of her cage (you open the door, pet her, give her some food, and wait for her to come out). "Don't be afraid, Mama," Ivy said. "Hold her," she demanded. She seemed to want Val to be afraid of Lemon, but Val wasn't.

Ivy took good care of Lemon and played with her, and when Val said, at the end of the visit, they could get a rat of their own, Ivy got as serious as a six-year-old can get. She said she liked Lemon a lot, but frankly, having a rat required a lot more work than having a dog. Unlike Kupa, their big apricot poodle, an area rug of a dog, Lemon needed special attention. You had to be careful around her, watch her. Ivy didn't feel ready for that kind of responsibility.

But then, when summer break came, once again Ivy wanted to take Lemon home.

It's possible most of her colleagues and many of her friends do not know how much Val enjoyed Lemon.

Lemon lived a good long life, and when she died, Ivy's school got Lemony and Snicket. (What is it with kids giving similar or the same names to animals?) Lemony and Snicket soon spent school vacations at Val's house.

I'm still waiting for Ivy to get her own rat. Maybe she never will. But I know that when she grows up, Ivy will always be a person who appreciates rats.

Once while I was out to dinner with three other women, all writers, we told one another things about ourselves that turned out to be as surprising as biting into a chocolate truffle that contains cayenne pepper.

Two of these women had known each other for a long time, and they seemed to enjoy reliving the story about how, when Ellen's son was young, Dorianne suggested a movie for him to watch. "Is it violent?" Ellen, the mother, wanted to know.

"Oh no," Dorianne had said. "It's great. He'll love it."

Turns out, *The Matrix* is a violent movie. By the time the main character, Neo, had wiped out a whole bunch of people, the now-troubled son came to his mom for comfort.

"I thought you said it wasn't violent," Ellen said.

"It isn't. Well, maybe a little. But it's not *real*." Dorianne tried to explain that from the perspective of the movie the action wasn't *really* taking place. In the movie, the real world is an illusion. For a scared little kid, that was a distinction without a difference.

So there we were, years later, laughing about how, when we are faced with something we consider art, we take from it what we want and are blind to aspects that others might find disturbing.

Then the mother of the poor *Matrix*-subjected son was revealed to be a champion killer of gophers. "Ellen's killed hundreds of them," said Dorianne, grinning.

I looked at this woman, a poet with the face of a smiling girl, a soft voice tinged with New Jersey but tempered by years in northern California, and could not believe it. I couldn't imagine her killing anything.

Then Ellen told a story about finding a dead mole and being so enchanted by the softness of the fur that she'd skinned it and made a dream catcher out of it to put above her son's bed (to ward off *Matrix*-inspired nightmares?).

You? I thought. *A mole skinner? You?*

The third woman, Ann, a novelist, had staples in her scalp from falling down at her daughter's school and bonking her head. She told a story about how, during the whole ordeal, as blood gushed through her hair and scared all the five-year-olds to whom she had brought cookies, all she could think about was that she wasn't wearing underwear that day and there she was, sprawled out on the floor.

So forgive me if I say when I confessed my next book was going to be a loving tribute to rats, I think I looked fairly normal in this crowd.

More so when it turned out two of the other women had also had rats as pets!

Dorianne, whose poems can make me feel punched in the gut—in a good way, if you can get your head around that—told about when her daughter's rat became sick, very sick. She drove to the vet, her daughter in the backseat, and held the rat against her neck. The rat, she knew, was dying. As she drove, she could feel his breath on her skin, feel his tiny heartbeat, and feel it slow. He died while she drove, died cradled in the warmth of her body. I could still see the loss on Dorianne's face; she had felt his death.

Ellen told about how, on a bored day, she and her kids

had decided to play beauty parlor, and they'd enticed the other neighborhood kids and mothers in for some hair brushing and nail polishing. They also decided, for reasons known only to mothers and kids who are imaginative and bored, that they would have a turbaned fortune-teller who would channel the thoughts of their rat Snowy. Snowy sat on her shoulder and squeaked into her ear.

The first woman to have her fortune told sat down. Snowy squeaked, and the turbaned translator said, "You will be contacted by someone you have lost."

The woman screamed, wailed, sobbed. Ran out. Her mother had died not six weeks before.

Spooked but still willing to continue, the next person came into the "booth."

Snowy did his squeaking and whispering and foretold that the woman would soon be going on a trip.

Yikes! She and her family had been planning a Hawaiian vacation.

Such were the adventures of Snowy the rat.

I had liked and admired these women, but now I knew we shared something few others would understand.

Behind closed doors tons of people like the motorcycle-riding family, like Val, like the poets Ellen and Dori-anne, love rats. People who had them as kids, or whose friends had them, or who were biology majors and worked with them in labs, or who are just, I don't know, enlightened.

As I mentioned earlier, the only times I thought it would be better to have two rats was when I had to travel. Though, in truth, it never occurred to me to get another one, as I was in love with Iris, not the idea of rats.

So I needed honeymunchkin sitters, especially during the winter break when I would be gone for three weeks with my mother while she had a stem-cell transplant.

It was my first year of teaching. I'd only just moved to Spokane, where I had few friends. One of my students, Ivory, already married with a child, had been a champion cheese taster in 4-H and wrote essays so beautiful they made me slightly jealous. Ivory agreed to take Iris when I went to upstate New York to stay with my mother while she was in the hospital.

During those rough few weeks, when doctors did a complete shutdown and reboot of my mother's immune system, I maintained a blog to keep her friends updated on the progress. Usually there wasn't much good to say. So I searched hard for uplifting tidbits.

Ivory would send me photos of Iris playing in a basket of

quilting scraps and monkeying around on Ivory's computer and I would post them, along with artificially perky reports on my mother's treatment. It was way more fun to write about Iris than about the bedsores on my mother's skin, the acrid smell of the hospital, the long runs I took in the cemetery to clear my head. Ivory, I wrote in one blog post, promised not to let her young daughter put Iris in her mouth, though she claimed Iris was much more hygienic than many of the things that went in that girl's mouth.

When I wrote to Ivory thanking her for the gazillionth time for taking care of Iris, she replied, "I'm glad that something that is so easy for me is so important to you."

I needed to express my gratitude because I think it's always important to do so: it never goes without saying that you appreciate what someone has done for you, no matter how little effort is required of them.

The next time I had to go away, Ivory had already graduated. I chose my second student-babysitter, Ellie, because she had a rabbit named Sequoia who was bigger than most cats and many dogs and I recognized her as someone who understands animals. When I asked her if she'd be willing to do Iris duty she said yes, she'd be happy to.

This is the note I left:

Rat whisperer,

I'm almost packed and ready to go. I just realized that I didn't get Iris any more organic broccoli, so be sparing with what's left in the fridge. I think she's still a bit porked out from the last time I left. I've put a lot of food in her cage (but I suspect she's been emptying it into stashes I can't find). If it looks like the bowl is empty, check her sleeping hut. If that's clean, give the hammock a squeeze. You're likely to feel the crumby remainders, but also some nuggets. If you can try to keep a good amount in there, that would be great. Also if you can keep an eye on the water levels. She seems to prefer to drink out of her litter-cage water bottle (go figure). Also, if she's been out for a while, plop her back in the litter cage for a pee. If she has to poop, she'll go in there herself (she likes to do her pooping in there when she can).

I recommend laps around the couch as a form of exercise. She'll chase you if you squeal and clap enough.

I'm going to try not to freak out. I know that you are a most excellent rodent caregiver, but I am, after all, still me.

Help yourself to any food or drink stuff you can scrounge. I stocked up on Cheez-Its (yum). There's lots of soda. And plenty of condiments. Feel free to live it up. Or if you want to cook a five-course dinner here, you're welcome to do so (as long as Iris is invited). There's a dearth of cooking utensils and pots, however.

Okay, I'm sure you have my cell, but here it is again. The vet is North Division Animal Hospital; number by the side of the little poochie's cage.

Thanks a zillion,
Rachel

While I was gone, I apparently got concerned, which is completely normal, right? So after a day—or maybe only a few hours—when I hadn't gotten a report I contacted Ellie to make sure everything was okay. Here's her response:

RT: It has come to my attention that I failed to update you about your darling baby. So here I go. I visited Iris on Thursday night and she was as cute as ever. She darted out of her cage and circled around our feet for a little while before I snatched her up and brought her to the couch, where she walked around my hands and lap for a bit. She chased around her toy rope and my scarf; she bolted into your bedroom. She hid in the soda box in the kitchen and came out to get some broccoli. Man, she is cute. She hung out on shoulders, and twirled, and hopped and scurried, and even went to the bathroom in her little cage-thing without being prompted. Linked up are a few photos. She misses you lots.

Peace,
Ellie

Can you look at this photo of baby rats without making squealing noises? I can't.

Get Thee to a Rattery

Where does a right-minded person acquire a rat?

I've already confessed that I got Iris at a pet store in the mall. I expect to receive some hate mail as a result of this unwitting transgression. As I said, mistakes were made (note how handy the passive voice is).

So where does a right-minded and caring individual who wants to bring a varmint into her life go to find one?

A rattery.

What, you might wonder, is a rattery?

I wondered too and wanted to visit one, until I learned that usually it's just a room in the house of someone who loves and breeds rats and has become, in the process, an amateur geneticist. Most of these folks maintain websites, which run the gamut from the beautifully designed and professionally written to simple just-the-facts bullet points and some cute photos.

Many give their owners' rat bona fides: membership in the North American Rat Registry, the American Fancy Rat & Mouse Association, the Rat & Mouse Club of America. Many note they *do not* sell rats for feeders (snakes). Many tell their own stories. A lot start the same way: with a pet-store rat who came home knocked up and rat owners who got savvy and educated themselves about breeding. There are photos, not only of the available adoptees, but also of the bucks and does. Interestingly, in the world of domestic rats, when bucks and does mate they have kittens. Wild rat babies are called pups. I can't pretend to understand this.

Here's a random list of ratteries, simply because the names alone say so much about the passionate people behind them:

Wolf Magic Rattery

Poke A Dot Rattery

Rat A Tat Rattery

Blue Skies Rattery

Black Wolf Rattery

Paradise Rockstar Rodentry!

So Licky Rattery

Rat Dippity Rattery

Twisted Tails Rattery

Ember of Passion Rattery

Oh Rats Rattery

Little Loves Rattery

Social Rats Adoption and Rescue

Roaming Rodents Rattery

Rat's Nest Rattery

Sweet Genes Rodentry

Willow Creek Rats

Ratty Rat Rattery

The 28th Rat

Three Peas Rattery

Topi Rats

AristoRats

Dark Passion Rattery

Here's the description from A Gothic Rattery, run by Aria, a twentysomething who lives in Florida with her parents, works in their restaurant, and studies American Sign Language.

A Gothic Rattery is a small home-based rattery in Gainesville, Florida. I strive for amazing personalities in my babies. A pet peeve of mine is unsocialized babies. I try my best to introduce my babies to new people, situations, smells, and sounds. I only breed healthy, friendly rats. Health and personalities are more important to me than looks. I have a few types I specifically breed, but my main goals focus on health. A few goals I am working on are: Recessive blazes (these are not high-white and are safe from Mega-Colon concerns), Seal-Point Siamese, nice curly rex, and Russian blue. My breeding stock come from my own lines of rats as well as from Ape's Little Paws Rattery (ALP), Ratley Crue (CRUE), Atlantic Beach Rattery (ABR), and The Menagerie (TMG), who have been kind enough to share their fantastic rats with me. Please read the Adoption Rules and Adoption Process pages below and check out the Current Litters page to find current information about babies.

Some of this may not be clear to you. When I first started looking into ratteries and talking to breeders in order to research this book, I was often confused. "Recessive blazes"? "High-white"? "Mega-Colon"? These words meant nothing to me. I was intimidated and overwhelmed by the amount I thought I had to learn. The idea of having to explain all of this made me want to stick my head in the oven. (Don't worry. I have an electric oven.)

Then I realized I've been a contented dog mother for more than twenty years and I couldn't tell you anything about the family tree of either of my mutts. I can't discern the breeds of some of the horses I ride and don't know one bird from another unless they're big and distinctive like bald eagles or tiny and annoying like hummingbirds. If you're looking for detailed information on the vast varieties of rats, there's tons of great stuff available and you're not going to get an in-depth treatment from me.

For now, we have to talk a little—just a little—about genetics.

Genes, you may already know, are bits of DNA that control an assortment of inheritable factors. Different types of the same gene, called alleles, make for variation. Normal people have earlobes that are attached. Others, like my mother, have lobes that hang down. That's because my mother and I got different alleles of the gene for earlobes. I spent a lot of time making fun of my mother's earlobes.

It's the alleles that give us variation in hair and eye color and account for the diversity you find in dogs, pigeons, and rats. It's also possible that different genes and their alleles can account for behavior. (Remember all that stuff about domestication from many chapters ago? That.)

So, within a litter of rats, a buffet of alleles accounts for lots of different types. The American Fancy Rat & Mouse Association (AFRMA) recognizes six varieties:

Standard: This is, not surprisingly, your basic rat with short, smooth, glossy hair.

Rex: These dudes have curly hair and whiskers. Not curly like poodles, but more wiry, like terriers; their coats look disheveled to me, like they've always just gotten out of bed and haven't yet brushed their hair.

Tailless: I'm guessing this needs no further explanation, except to say that, like Manx cats, the seeming appeal of having a rat without a tail is balanced by the fact that they are prone to lots of health problems.

Hairless: It takes a special person to love a hairless rat. They look like ET or newborn humans and require almost as much extra TLC to keep them warm. Owners must use baby wipes or massage them with extra-virgin olive oil so that their skin doesn't dry out.

Satin: This confuses me. Satin rats are supposed to have coats that are even more lustrous, thinner, and longer than your standard rat's. They are kind of the prom queens of ratdom. I don't know for certain, but I wonder if Iris was satin. I mean, her fur was so soft, so shiny, so beautiful—or maybe that was because I loved her.

Dumbo: Peek again at the rat on the cover of this book. That is a Dumbo rat. These guys look more like teddy bears, with big, round ears set far back on their heads. You can think of them as the gateway drugs to rat addiction.

But wait, that's not all. In addition to those six main varieties, there are different color and body markings, as well as thirty-three distinct and recognized colors. That's a lot of variability in rats.

Self rats have bodies that are entirely one color. They are: beige, black, blue, blue-beige, champagne, chocolate, cocoa, lilac, mink, platinum, Russian blue, Russian dove, sky blue, black-eyed white, or pink-eyed white.

AOC stands, believe it or not, for "any other color." The whole bodies of these rats are the same color, but the coats consist of individual hairs banded with two or more colors and evenly interspersed with colored "guard" hairs. The colors are: agouti, amber, blue agouti, chinchilla, cinnamon, cinnamon pearl, fawn, lynx, pearl, Russian blue agouti. Agouti is the color of wild rats. Your subway scurriers and apartment infesters are agouti, which means that each of their hairs has bands of different colors.

AOCP (any other color pattern) rats have a combination of two or more colors other than white arranged in a recognized pattern. They can be: blue point Siamese, Burmese, Himalayan, Russian blue point Siamese, seal point Siamese, and merle. These guys tend to have darker "points," on their face, ears, nose, and feet, like Siamese cats. Silvered rats' coats are evenly interspersed with white hairs. They include: silver black, silver blue, silver chocolate, silver fawn, silver lilac, and silver mink.

That's a lot, right? There's more.

Now we get to the complication of marked rats.

Here's the AFRMA breakdown. These are groups named according to the pattern of their markings, in any recognized color:

> **English Irish** have a white equilateral triangle on the chest.

> **Irish** have a moderately sized, evenly shaped white marking on the belly, four white feet, and a white tail tip.

> **Berkshires** have a completely white belly, white feet, white tail, and a small white spot between the ears.

> **Essexes** have markings similar to Berkshires, but the color fades gently to white.

> **Variegateds** have a colored head and shoulders, a white blaze on the forehead, small and numerous color splashes from shoulders to tail, including on the sides and tail, and a white belly.

Blazes have a white wedge-shaped blaze on the face from muzzle to ears. This appears only in Berkshires or Variegateds.

Dalmatians have numerous color splashes distributed over the entire body with no solid clear-cut markings on a white body.

Hoodeds have a white body with a colored hood to cover head, neck, chest, and shoulders, and a spine marking extending from hood to tail in an unbroken, moderately wide stripe without ragged edges or brindling.

Barebacks have a colored hood to cover head, neck, chest, and shoulders on a white body.

Cappeds have a white body with a colored cap on the head not extending to the throat or past the ears.

Maskeds have a white body and a colored "mask" across the face and around the eyes.

Not surprisingly, **odd-eye** rats have one eye
that is pink and one eye that is dark ruby or
black. They may be in any recognized color
and any recognized or unrecognized marking.

And **unstandardized** rats are also exactly what
you'd expect.

This kind of complicated categorization will be familiar to
anyone who has gotten deep into horses or dogs, or even
to those of us who have gone to the livestock exhibits at the
state fair and skimmed the surface of all the different strains
there are of rabbits, or sheep, or chickens.

Each of these colors and traits is the result of a gene.
Rat breeders, even beginners, can learn to select for them
and specialize in a certain type of rat. Many choose to try
to keep that Dumbo gene front and center. A rounder rat
is a cuter rat, and there's no question the Dumbos are
cute.

Reputable breeders, like any of us of decent character,
will be most concerned with the health and safety of their
charges. A standard "adoption agreement" might read:
"This rat is adopted first and foremost as a companion animal and family member and is to be cared for as such. The

rat is to live with humans in the buyer's living quarters or in such living arrangement agreed upon by both the seller and buyer."

Fancy rat people tend to be adamant that their efforts do not go toward making big bulges in the bellies of snakes. They want recognition of the bloodlines with the initials of their rattery before the name when their offspring are going to shows. They mostly don't want too much money; rat breeding does not have a big profit margin.

On its website AFRMA lists the following questions for potential rat owners to answer:

1. Are you willing to spend a minimum of a half hour a day with your pet?

2. Are you willing to clean its cage once a week or more often if necessary?

3. Are you prepared to go out of your way to obtain the correct bedding and food for your pet?

4. Have you bought and read at least one book about rats or mice?

5. Will you take your rat or mouse to a veterinarian should it become ill?

6. Will you check your pet's food and water at least once a day to be sure it has both in adequate supply?

7. Have you thought about who will care for your rat or mouse when you go on vacation?

8. Are you prepared to spend at least $60 on an initial cage setup for your pet rat, $30 for your pet mouse?

9. If you are the parent of a child who wants a pet rat or mouse, are you willing to accept responsibility for seeing that the animal is properly cared for, and care for it yourself when the need arises? (Children under fifteen should not be expected to take full responsibility for a pet.)

10. Are you prepared to accept *full* responsibility for your pet for its *entire* life?

The people who breed rats do it as a passion. They're not in it to get rich, and they love to share their excitement and their information.

There are also rat rescue operations, like Tori's. She kept all of her rats, but others are willing to adopt out most of theirs to good families. Many rats are "surrendered" by folks who take them home but then decide they can no longer care for them. Or they move and can't take the rats along. Or they end up with unexpected litters. The people who take them in get to know the personality of each rat and are great resources to help families find the right fit. They often have a return policy. If you find you're not the right person to have a rat, the rescuers will let you bring it back without shaming you. They can give advice on care, will recommend vets, and will be happy to talk to you for hours about your beloved little darling.

I always said Iris was a hooded rat. That's because I didn't know better.

Once I started looking into the different varieties of rats, I got more overwhelmed than I do in a fancy ice-cream store. I'm used to Ben & Jerry's and Baskin-Robbins. I know my favorite flavors. Mint chocolate chip is, of course, the best, and, as everyone knows, it has to be fluorescent green. But when you go to the boutique ice-cream shops, you enter a complicated world where you have to decide if you want lavender ginger or cardamom or house-paint flavor.

What was Iris? Was I calling her the equivalent of plain vanilla when she was really Tahitian bean?

Then I got an idea.

I sent a message to Mary Giles, a rat breeder in England who had been particularly kind and helpful to me, and said, "Hey, if I show you pictures of my rat Iris, can you tell me what color she is?"

Mary responded right away: "Most probably—bearing in mind there can be photograph/screen colour inaccuracies."

So I sent off a photo. Or rather, three photos, because I mean, seriously, who wouldn't want to look at Iris? She was so beautiful.

Mary said, "She was a mismarked agouti, and I'd opt for variegated—sweet girl."

What?

"Mismarked?" I replied. "That's hard for an overachieving mom to hear!"

Mary's response was immediate, and warm, "Mismarked only in terms of the (UK) showing standard for variegated—there should be more coloured spots over her back . . . but quite right, as her mum, she was perfect."

Mary understood.

Who could be afraid of this?

This Is How Grief Works

How do you survive the death of a loved one?

On February 3, 2009, my mother died.

My relationship with my mother was singular, unique to us. Other daughters may refer to the one who spawned them as the CLM, the Cute Little Mother, but mine was the cutest. Perhaps it was common, in the late seventies, for teenage girls and their maternal units to eat two-pound bags of peanut M&M'S while watching *The Love Boat* and then complain to each other for hours about how sick they felt. Maybe everyone goes to the Clinique counter at department stores and draws clown faces on each other with expensive makeup, or blacks out their teeth with pieces of food and grins like monkeys at the waitstaff in fancy restaurants, and then laughs until they pee themselves. I'm sure I'm not the only one who would think about how much I loved and missed my mother, and then call her, only to take umbrage at a passing remark and sulk like a sixth grader. But still, no one ever loved her mommy exactly the way I did.

In an email to me after my mother died, a friend who had overheard one of our daily check-ins in my Bluetooth-enabled car said he thought often about the way she and I had interacted—how easy and fun the conversation was, how we seemed like such good friends.

For four and a half years my mother thought she could beat an incurable disease. For four and a half years we never talked about her death. A longtime deployer of strategic denial, she kept saying she just wanted to get better, to feel like herself again. The notion that this might never happen was not entertained or mentioned.

My mother died almost exactly on the schedule she thought she'd heard from her doctor. When I talked to him, he said he never told her she had only three weeks left to live. I knew enough about him—and medicine—to believe this. But after four years of thinking she could beat an unbeatable disease, my mother finally understood she was going to die. In her last few weeks, the CLM felt better than she had in years. She had an amazing network of friends, and she got to spend time with them and laugh, to be her unstoppable, playful, vigorous self.

She wanted to die at home. She did not want to go back into the hospital. She wanted me, not my brother, to have the medical power of attorney to make decisions for her because she believed I understood what she would want. She did not want any kind of memorial service or ceremony. She wanted to know I would be okay. I lied and told her I would be.

During those last weeks we had the best, hardest conversations. I got to tell her what a good mother she had been, how having her believe in me and my abilities gave me the confidence to do daunting things. I apologized for my chronic impatience, for not being a better daughter, for making fun of her detached earlobes. We talked about everything: her life, her death, her wishes, her fears. She worried about me, knowing that when I hurt I withdraw. She fretted that the tenuous link between my brother and me would be frayed.

After my mother died, friends and acquaintances wanted to tell me what to expect. "This is how grief works," the most pedantic of them would say. And then I'd get a prescription, a laundry list, a series of steps.

My well-intentioned friends said to me: *You will get more tired than you realize and then will be less able to deal with things. It will hit you in waves, unexpected tsunamis of pain. It will be an avalanche; you never know what will trigger something catastrophic. It's a process. It's a part of life. It will pass.*

The day after my mother died, when I was felled by a migraine and could not get out of bed, a friend brought me breakfast: a granola bar, a Vicodin, and instructions not to take the painkiller on an empty stomach. This was useful. Nothing else helped, except having my beloved Iris cuddled next to me.

The only thing more upsetting than having people tell me how I would feel was listening to them talk about their own dead mothers. Of course I knew people liked to share stories of illness, death, and grief. I understood that. But those conversations were like a game of jacks, where there's no interaction, just a taking of turns. In my sadness and hurt I didn't want to sit through their turn. My love for my mother was mine alone; why couldn't my grief be as well?

I lost weight and joked that I was on the Dead Mother Diet. I parried concerned messages with brusque reassurances. For a while I said I was enjoying the "denial phase" of grief and hoped it would last forever.

And at night, in the dark, I'd sometimes wake with a start because I thought I heard my mom's voice calling my name. I had dreams where she wasn't dead, and when she came back, she had no place to go, no clothes, no car. She needed a car, though she hadn't been able to drive for years.

No one would ever say, "This is how love works." We've all read enough literature, seen enough movies, to know that would be silly.

Sometimes I wonder whether if I were more open to the opinions of others, more susceptible to pop psychologizing, that time would have been easier for me. If I could have reassured myself that everything I was feeling and thinking was typical and normal, would that have helped? I doubt it. The only way I got through those first motherless months was with the help of friends who would listen to me talk and keep their ideas, opinions, and experiences to themselves; numbing painkillers at the right times; and the memories of the specific ways in which I loved my Cute Little Mother. If I ever hear anyone say to me again, "This is how grief works," I will kick them in the shins. Hard.

Three months after my mother died, Iris began to ail.

My sweet baby had for a while been showing signs of age, signals I couldn't acknowledge. I knew Iris was skinny.

When she was young, I watched her weight and made sure her snacks were healthy and not full of empty calories. Obesity, I knew, is the quickest way to shorten an animal's life, so I have always been strict about the weight of my pets. But for nearly a year Iris had been skinny and so I gave her as many treats as she wanted, including chocolate (which is good for rats) and peanut butter.

Iris didn't move as well as she used to and couldn't climb with her former relish. She slept more, wanted to cuddle more, needed to be held. Her fur was no longer as silky; she spent less time grooming.

Addled by the loss of my mother, I lay in bed with Iris and told her over and over how much I loved her.

Then one day when I went to let her out for our morning ritual, I found my baby hunched in pain. For the first time ever, Iris wouldn't leave her cage.

A veterinarian friend once told me something I'll never forget. When it comes to making the hard decision to put an animal to sleep, she said, no one ever does it too soon. Most people wait too long and let their animals suffer unnecessarily.

As I watched my mother grow sicker, her pain becoming more constant and more severe, I vowed to myself I would not force Iris to go through that. One of the things we get to do for animals is put them out of their misery, even if it means increasing ours. Until I watched my mother suffer through the last years of her life, sat by helpless as she spent her days in agony, her nights nauseated, unable to enjoy any of the things she had loved so much, I didn't know what misery looked like. Now I know.

From the time I got Iris as a tiny five-week-old, I thought about her death. After her first birthday I stopped having parties for her. Most rats live two years. When Iris turned three, time felt borrowed. She had the highest pain threshold of anyone I've ever known. Friends who didn't realize they needed to watch where they put their feet in our house had stepped on her tail. A kid had once knocked her off my shoulder to the floor. She had endured a couple of surgeries. Through all that she soldiered on, never complaining. When I saw her that morning, I knew.

At three years and five months, old for a rat but nowhere near long enough for me, I took Iris to the vet for the last time.

Helen the vermin-chasing felon

Moving On

Does having a rat ruin you for other pets?

Because I knew people do crazy things after the death of a parent—like marrying the wrong guy—I imposed a yearlong dating moratorium on myself.

It lasted eight months. Then I met someone and we got into a relationship. His kindness and generosity made it easy to be together, except when we disagreed about politics or issues of social justice. We did fun things, including lots of hiking and camping and binge-watching episodes of *Project Runway*. He wore a dorky apron over his jeans and T-shirt when he cooked, but since he acted as my personal chef and made my favorite foods, I tried not to make fun of him. He cleaned the house and mothered me, which was wonderful when it didn't feel smothering.

After we'd been together for about a year, we went camping in the Bitterroot Mountains of western Montana. I started talking about how much I missed Iris. His dead wife had been an expert on bats and they'd had a pet bat. We both missed living with animals.

I surprised myself by saying, "I want a dog."

"Let's get a dog," he said as we clipped along the trail, as if it were no bigger a deal than picking up some ice cream on the way home.

I was marching in front—I always have to be in front—and stopped dead. He hiked right into me. I turned to look at him.

"Really?"

"Why not?"

"Okay, but if"—I said *if*, and I knew it was more like *when*—"we break up, there can be no custody battles. The dog will be mine."

"Fine."

"I'll be in charge of all dog decisions."

We started hiking again.

"No problem."

"The dog sleeps on the bed."

He didn't respond right away. I could hear him breathing, could hear his footfalls behind me.

"Fine," he said, finally. "But not on the couch. I don't want dog hair on the couch."

The trail became a series of switchbacks up the mountain and I walked faster and thought for a while. We lived mostly in his house, though I had kept my own place. I realized I needed to be able to compromise on some things.

"I want a female."

"Bitch," he said.

"What?"

"Female dog. A bitch," he said, and I could hear him giggle a little.

At the end of the hike, we returned to camp and he cooked us pasta while I lay in the hammock and pretended to read a book. My heart pounded as I realized: I'm going to get a dog!

And then it took months.

I made weekly trips to the three local animal shelters. I'd walk down the row of cages and cast a quick glance and mutter to myself, "Not you, not you, not you." I didn't feel guilty about not wanting to take everyone home. I knew how big a commitment having a dog was and knew, too, that fit mattered more than anything else.

I did not want a puppy. I had a long list of requirements, in fact, about what I wanted and did not want. Not a puppy.

One day I went to the Spokane Humane Society and it was teeming with puppies. Two litters had just been brought in. I looked at them and then poked around to ask if anyone knew anything about these adorable wigglers.

A volunteer gave me the lowdown on one of the litters. The mama dog had gotten knocked up and then arrested and sent to the pokey (the Humane Society). Two weeks before the dog gave birth the volunteer had taken the expectant mother home. This no-nonsense woman had cared for the puppies for the first eight weeks of their lives and would, she said, be happy to answer my questions.

I told her what I was looking for and started rattling off the list of what I didn't want. It included:

> Not too big
> Not too small
> Not shaggy
> Not slobbery
> Not a barker
> Not stupid-happy
> Not a black dog (no good reason)
> Not a white dog (ditto)

Not a purebred

Not a neurotic

No floppy ears

No smushed-in face

The list of what I wanted included:

Smart

Athletic

Adventuresome

Adaptable

Good sense of humor

Smart

Smart

Smart

The woman looked at me and said, "I've raised five hundred puppies. This is the best litter I've ever seen and this is the dog for you." She pointed to a particular pup, who was not even the most attractive of the bunch. She said this female was a thinker: curious, but also cautious. She was really, really smart.

Have I mentioned that I did not want a puppy?

"These dogs are going to go fast," the woman said. "They

were just spayed and neutered and this is the first day they've been available for adoption."

She put the puppy and me in a small room together so we could get acquainted. As she'd mentioned, the little mutt proved a careful explorer. She was delightful, with a round face and ears folded in half, a patch of caramel-colored fur around one eye. The other part of her face was white, and she had freckles on her head and snout. Her markings weren't as flashy as those of her siblings; next to them she seemed kind of washed out. I looked for reasons to cross her off the list, terrified of making a bad decision.

But other than the fact that she was a puppy, she seemed perfect, the embodiment of what I said I sought.

I called my boyfriend and told him Stella and I would be home soon. He was surprised but enthusiastic. Enthusiasm was another of his good qualities.

Each time I've imagined myself with a pet, I've given her a name. Each time I've brought a pet home, I've realized the name I chose didn't work. Though I adore the name Stella, this dog was not Stella. Plus, I realized you can't scream out that name without someone thinking you're Marlon Brando in *A Streetcar Named Desire*.

After a few days of trying on different names, the right one came to me. I named my puppy after my great-aunt, a woman who had influenced me and loved me, and whom I admired for her fierceness and her smarts. She had been a chief petty officer in the Coast Guard, had left her family in New York and moved to California, had been married a couple of times, and had ultimately chosen to live alone. When she was old I'd visited her in Florida during spring break in college and we had a blast. She encouraged me to be independent and strong.

Helen.

Believe it or not, it didn't occur to me until much later how close that name was to Hannah, my previous dog. Not until I had called Helen Hannah a couple of times did I figure that out.

Just as I have a type when it comes to naming, so too do I go for similar-looking dogs. Helen is about the same size Hannah was, around fifty pounds, though Helen is more muscular and athletic. Helen's ears folded in half until she got older and then they stood straight up: giant triangular antennae. People always comment on what big ears she has, just as a totally different group of people said the same thing about Hannah. Helen's contrast color is identical to the reddish blond that covered all of Hannah's body. Both dogs were more pointy than round.

People rarely asked me about Hannah—they assumed she

was just a mutt—but I can't walk down the street attached to Helen without folks stopping me and inquiring what kind of dog she is. At first I wondered if this signaled something funny. Did they think she was a dangerous pit bull? Some think she looks pit-ish. Others say dingo, as if wild dogs from Australia are running around the streets of Spokane impregnating the local gals. People often think she is mostly Australian cattle dog (the freckles on her head are called "ticking"), though her coat is shorter and silkier, her legs longer, and her snout pointier than a red heeler's. Why did so many people ask me about her lineage?

Now I'm used to it and I know it's because, in my completely unbiased opinion, she's stunning and unusual-looking. I have come to expect to hear "That's a beautiful dog" before or after I'm asked what breed she is.

But whereas Hannah was a worrier and kept careful watch on me and those she loved, Helen acts like a teenage boy, even at age five. She's got a mischievous sense of humor and likes to tease and taunt me, especially by snatching my slippers and then bashing me with them. I pay her back by doing some teasing of my own: "Is that a cat out there? I think I see a cat!" She falls for it every time and runs to the back door with her Mohawk up.

During her puppyhood the boyfriend was in charge of

letting her out at night and early in the morning. He cleaned up her messes and tolerated her lying between us in bed. She nestled against me and shoved her four paws painfully into his back. The three of us took baths in his giant Jacuzzi tub, and there, I'm afraid, I instilled in Helen a love of water I regret every time we pass a mud puddle. The boyfriend did everything right, but we kept fighting about his fondness for Fox News and Latinate verbs. He liked to use words like *fabricate* instead of *make* and didn't believe me when I pointed out they meant exactly the same thing. We broke up.

Helen and I moved out, into a house with a big fenced-in backyard and a nearby trail on which we could run and hike. She's an excellent runner and in her first official race, the Snow Joke Half Marathon, held in Montana in February on a course of ice and snow (it's no joke—get it?), she came in fourth dog out of more than forty. She would have preferred to ditch me and go with the fast guys, as she does when we run with groups, but that wasn't an option. So instead she pulled me for 13.1 miles trying to beat the pack. We also go skijoring, a real sport, where she wears a harness and actually tows me as I struggle to stay upright on cross-country skis.

Helen is brave but careful, interested in all people. She is brainy and athletic, and I get lots of praise just by walking down the street with her. To the outside world she looks well adjusted; I bring her with me to class because she loves students. "Do you want to go see the students?" I ask, and she rushes to the door. They love her and call her an academic stress reliever.

She's not perfect. No one knows how mopey she can get when we're at home and she's bored. No one sees her when I tell her we're going in the car and she decides she doesn't like where I say we're going. No one sees her snatching my Ugg slippers and refusing to give them up until I am nearly in tears. When she's not getting enough attention, she'll grab one of her nine hundred toys and squeak it, loudly and repeatedly, in my face. Or she'll clobber me with a paw while I sit at the computer. If I don't respond, she'll nail me with the other one.

I am complicit here. I tell her every day how special she is, and some of my rules are lax. If I'm eating something, she gets a bite. Sometimes she gets more than a bite. I sleep on a sliver of the bed because she spends all night pushing me toward the edge, leaving me tired and sore. I let her do this because it delights me to feel her weight against me, to wake up with her face near mine on the pillow.

Helen, for all her captivating qualities, is also unfortunately a brutish predator. Her scorecard as of this writing:

Wins

3 4 squirrels (she nailed another one just after I finished this manuscript)

9 marmots (they're like squirrels on steroids. bulkier but not as fast)

Losses

1 skunk

2 porcupines

Ties

2 porcupines

If you say certain words in Helen's presence—she's always eavesdropping on conversations that are none of her business—she will perk up her ginormous nosy ears, ready to look for vermin with a murderous glint in her eye or excited that someone is coming over. If you gave her a vocabulary test consisting of, say, the words *cat, dog, squirrel, marmot, porcupine, turkey, horse, toy, new toy, Frosty, Teddy, Bunny, Tick, Elephant, Banana, ball, big blue ball, good rawhide, regular rawhide, treat, eat, hungry, dinner, breakfast, chicken, steak, downstairs, upstairs, up, down, under the couch, on the table, Kong, car, backseat, drive, drink, swim, pool, water, kiss, hug, high five, look, see, walk, run, ski, couch, chair, bed, covers, under, move, you gotta move!, you know*

you gotta move!, *Sancho, Nadine, Roxy, Greg, Chris, John,*
Missoula, Sage, David, Becky, Staci, students, former stu-
dents, Bachelorettes, she'd ace it.

Often I'll invite her to come close to me so I can tell her
something. I'll say, "Come here. I want to tell you something."

She comes and sits ready to hear.

Then I'll ask her for a hug.

She'll put her paws around my neck.

"Kiss?"

She'll lick my face.

I'll say, "You know who's coming over?"

She'll cock her head to the side waiting to hear the
answer.

I'll say, "Chris! Chris is coming over."

She'll jump up, wag her tail, and rush to the front window, where she'll perch on what we call her tuffet (like Little
Miss Muffet's) and wait for our visitor to show up.

Or I'll say, "Do you want to go see the students?"

I always know the answer to that one. Just as I know what
will happen if I say "We have to go in the car."

Then she'll get all sulky, unless I tell her we're going
somewhere she wants to go, like to school, or to a trailhead
for a run, or even to spend three hours driving to Missoula
to see her best dog friend, Nadine. If I say we're going to the
grocery store, she won't even raise her head.

The tricks she can learn are limited only by my ability to come up with new ideas. She can sit, stay, lie down, give a high five, leap, leap over my leg, do a figure eight between my legs, back up like a crab, bark, turn on and off the light switch, twirl, twirl while standing, run around the chair, play dead when you point a finger at her and say bang, do yoga (downward facing dog), and cover her face with her paw.

She rarely barks except when we're on the bed playing the game called Man Overboard. I say the words "Man overboard!" or just start to say, really slowly, "Maaaaaaaan," and she braces herself and shoves her butt at me. I gently put my feet on that cute butt and prepare to punt her off the bed. Or try to. Usually I can't do it: she's learned to make herself immovable. When I catch her off balance and she leaps to the floor, she'll issue a sharp bark. It means *Phooey! You got me this time, but just you wait.* Helen, her mother's dog, doesn't like to lose.

Despite some criminal tendencies and the competitive streak that causes her to drop me at the back of the pack to run with the fast guys in front, I dote on Helen.

But for a long time after I brought that eight-week-old Buddha-bellied wiggler home I wondered if I would ever love this dog as much as I loved my rat Iris.

In many ways, Iris was a lot easier to love.

The logo for the rat fest in Seattle created by
Lynn Rosskamp, a breeder in Washington State

Ratapalooza

What does a celebration of rats look like?

People in my town sometimes stop me on the street to declare, "Hey, you're Rachel Toor."

When I ask if I know them, they say no, but they recognize Helen, who's usually attached to me by a leash.

Yes, I've turned my dog into something of a celebrity. I post zillions of photographs of her on social media; she's way more recognizable and photogenic than I am. People are either bored or they're interested in Helen. They post pictures of their own dogs or send me videos of dogs doing funny things.

Some people are, of course, afraid of dogs, or prefer cats,

or don't like animals. Helen seeks these folks out, even though I tend not to trust them. She'll lie at their feet and drape a paw over their shoes. She'll sit facing them and then slowly crawl into their laps and start licking their faces. She's a fifty-pound missionary for doghood. If you think you don't like dogs, she will try to convert you to the canine cause, and maybe squish you a little in the process.

Nothing about my love for Helen is hard for other people to understand, except maybe its intensity. Even if you don't like dogs, you know many people who do. You may know other doting dog mamas. You may even be one. Most people don't need a couple hundred pages to tell them why dogs make great pets.

Iris was a far more lovable creature than Helen, and yet I always had to make a case for her, to explain to doubters how wonderful she was. Hence, this book, which I've been working on for more than a decade.

Like many authors, I find it difficult to write.

Wait. That might be an understatement.

Let me try to put it more clearly.

Like many authors, I would rather walk across a field of broken glass dodging flaming arrows than work on a book. Or would find it more fun to clean a public toilet with a toothbrush than sit down at my computer to face a blank page.

A good strategy to avoid writing but not seem like a slacker is to do research. Once I decided I wanted to write the flip side of *Rats*, I began to collect all the information I could find—any shiny bits, any juicy morsels—and soon I had stacks of books, tattered copies of journal articles, hundreds of saved links, and tons of emails from my friends alerting me to good rat material.

I went to the University of Chicago and met with Peggy Mason and Inbal Ben-Ami Bartal, the women whose experiment showed that rats feel empathy. I drove down to Pullman, to Washington State University, to meet with Jaak Panksepp, the rat tickler. When I described what I was interested in, Jaak suggested I get in touch with a neuroscientist at Virginia's Randolph-Macon College, Kelly Lambert.

Was I glad I did! I called Kelly and we talked like long-lost sisters from another mister. When I wrote my novel, I based one of the characters, a scientist, on a mash-up of Peggy, Inbal, and Kelly. I felt an instant connection with these supersmart researchers, warm women who cared deeply about their students (and their rats).

The next best thing after getting to talk to Kelly was learning she had a book coming out. If you like rats (and I'm going to assume at this point if you're still reading that you do), get yourself a copy of *The Lab Rat Chronicles: A Neuroscientist Reveals Life Lessons from the Planet's Most Successful Mammals*. In the introduction Kelly writes, "These unassuming little animals can teach us some essential lessons about how we, as humans, can lead successful lives. From emotional resilience and a strong work ethic to effective parenting and staying healthy, the lab rat is an unlikely but powerful role model for us all."

Don't you love her already? I always said I wanted a bracelet that read "WWID? What Would Iris Do?" Kelly wrote the book that explains all the ways in which that makes sense. She describes, in fun and accessible language, tons of cool experiments that will make you want to spend your days and nights learning science.

Kelly covered all of the lab-rat bases in ways I could never hope to and I realized I didn't have to write thing one about the science being done with rats. Every day it seems there are reports of new research; all you have to do is watch for them. Kelly's book gives you the big picture behind all of this exciting work.

Many of my friends (and even strangers) who knew of my rodent jones sent me articles about naked mole rats. These critters make the news a lot because, well, they're remarkable. They can live up to thirty years and don't get cancer.

They don't feel pain. They live in colonies ruled over by queens (like bees). But they are neither moles nor rats, so while I'd like to tell you more of the stuff that makes them so fascinating, they don't belong here.

For a while, I didn't think I could write the book I wanted to write without going to Tanzania. No, silly, not to climb Mount Kilimanjaro (okay, well maybe that *too*), but because I was desperate to meet the folks at HeroRATs, a program of the nonprofit organization APOPO, founded by Bart Weetjens, a Buddhist monk from Belgium.

The HeroRATs are giant Gambian pouched rats. They are far bigger than Iris was, though they still weigh less than a gallon of milk, and the folks at APOPO train them to do certain kinds of tricky detective work. For example, they tread softly over the ground to find—but not set off—unexploded land mines in Tanzania, Mozambique, Thailand, Angola, and Cambodia. Unlike dogs, who are more expensive to maintain and only work with one trainer, the rats will perform their duties no matter who's in charge. They live eight to ten years. These oversized rats have also learned to detect pulmonary tuberculosis in human spit quicker than and as accurately as microscopic tests.

I really, really, really wanted to go to Tanzania and meet these heroic workers. Of course I harbored thoughts of smuggling one home with me, maybe a retiree whose bomb-sniffing days were over. However, I also wanted to narrow the focus of this book to domesticated Norway rats who live as pets.

The big problem was that while I started working on this book with Iris resting on my lap, or balancing on my shoulder, or chasing my fingers as they pounded on the keyboard, after she died I found it painful to keep going. That's part of why it took me so long to finish. Grief has a way of blocking productivity.

When I adopted Helen and discovered her unfortunately predatory nature, I realized I wouldn't be able to get another rat, so I put the project on hold for a while and turned to other things.

Eventually I started reading about rats again. I joined Facebook groups about rat breeding, rat genetics, and rat care, watched seven thousand rat videos, and oohed and ahhed over social media photos of these adorable critters.

Then I needed a fix of soft fur and tiny starlike hands. I needed to hold a rat. I hunted down people in Spokane who had them as pets.

Marilyn teaches environmental science at a local community college. We met at a track workout and we often chatted as we jogged between intervals. Then she'd take off and kick my butt. And the butts of most of the men. Marilyn is very fast.

She's also had rats for a long time. She and her two sons had Shadow and Spotlight. They weren't, Marilyn said, the friendliest rats—they were a little shy, a little skittish—but she loved them. When I had dinner at their house, we took the rats out and let them wander around the table while we ate. It was nice to see someone else who didn't mind sharing her salad with vermin.

Dorian was a former student. When I found out he had rats I asked if I could come visit. Sure, he said.

His girlfriend Mariah had introduced him to the rat world. Mariah had grown up with rats and told me about a cat she'd had who'd learned how to open the rat cage. One of the rats would come out of the cage and climb on the back of the cat, and they'd hang out around the house. As Mariah told the story I put my hand to the rat cage. Sarah Jane came right over and started licking my finger. Then she climbed onto my hand. I petted the top of her head and her fur felt frizzy. It felt, in fact, a lot like my hair. Mariah said, "She's a rex. See how curly her whiskers are?"

It looked as if her whiskers had been singed in a fire.

Sarah Jane was agouti, the color of nature. She looked like

she could be wild, except that she had a white belly and white feet. She was not the most beautiful rat I'd ever seen (Iris was that, of course). She was, however, irresistible. I embarrassed myself in front of my former student and his girlfriend by telling Sarah Jane I loved her within seconds of our meeting. So not cool. But I couldn't help it. She was lovable. A total winner.

Mariah nodded, having seen it all before. "She's our ambassador. It doesn't take long for people who say they don't like rats to be won over by her."

Anastasia had two kids, a dog, a gynecologist husband, and an increasing number of rats. I got to meet them at a party and hid out with the rats instead of socializing with the people. Danielle was a graduate student who had a couple of her own. The problem was, I didn't know either of them well enough to be able to say to them, "Hey, I want to come over because I need rat time."

However, I did know my former student Ellie—one of Iris's rat sitters—quite well. She now worked for a software company and was living in Seattle with her filmmaker partner, Jonah.

Ellie and I decided we could attend Ratapalooza on World Rat Day, which is, in case you didn't know it, April 4. Ellie decided to adopt two baby girl rats. Jonah was less enthusiastic, but he had loved Iris (because, he said, Iris had loved him, which was true).

As you already know, Helen isn't one of those dogs who always want to go. Yet when I said, "We're going to see Ellie!" though Helen had only met her once, she was psyched. I didn't mention the four-hour drive.

Five hours later (I hadn't accounted for Seattle traffic) we arrived at Ellie and Jonah's tiny house in the über-groovy Ballard neighborhood. We got Thai takeout and went to a bar that allowed you not only to bring in food but also dogs. Helen went to her first bar! Mostly she stayed under the long table and patrolled for dropped scraps. However, my flirtatious dog also went over to a guy she'd just met, climbed into his lap, and gave him a big wet kiss. Then we had to have a discussion about appropriate bar behavior.

The next day, Ellie, Jonah, and I went to Ratapalooza. Ellie had already ordered a big cage, a water bottle, a bag of litter, and a travel cage. We expected to come home with two rat babies.

And I was expecting to get a lot of good rat material at Ratapalooza. I'd been reading about it on Facebook, and Ellie and I had been talking about it and looking forward to the event for months. I have to say I was disappointed when we got to the Ballard Community Center and saw only signs for an Easter egg hunt. The lawn was lousy with happy, sugar-drunk children. Inside the center was a room full of bunnies. We looked around, obviously confused, until a woman asked, "Are you here for the rats?"

"Yes!" Ellie, Jonah, and I said in unison.

"They're over there," she said, and pointed us to a room that looked like a middle-school gym.

We each paid our five-dollar entrance fee. Tables set up in a rectangle offered hammocks for sale, rat jewelry, and liteRATure. As we entered we heard an announcement calling for the longest tail contest.

"No longest tails?" the announcer said.

No competitors.

We did get to see the rat race. It took place in a Plexiglas structure divided into five lanes and covered with a plastic top. Competitive rat owners placed their athletes at one end and expected them to run to the other.

These rat experts didn't seem to take into account the social nature of their contestants. Each rat got into the lane, and then after a few steps returned to his or her owner. One guy got nearly to the end but then flipped to scamper back to the hands of his person.

The rat show went from eleven a.m. to four p.m. Ellie had wanted to arrive early because she feared there would be no babies left. Jonah and I thought she was crazy and we took our time getting ready. Ellie was right. By the time we got there, just after eleven thirty, the only two adoptable baby girls had been nabbed. Two young women had already filled out an application for them. The owner told Ellie if the women didn't pass, she could apply.

What, you may wonder, does it take to pass a rat adoption test? Unfortunately I still don't know. Whatever it was, they passed and they snagged the babies.

Another rescue had a bunch of rats, but they were mostly males. Ellie wanted females (rat balls). They were also older. One particularly sweet girl acted, the rescuer said, like a puppy, even though she was eighteen months old. Eighteen months, we knew, was beyond middle age for a rat. She was a delight, though, and it was hard to leave her there.

We held a hairless rat who at first looked larval but because of her outgoing personality became terribly attractive, and a rex who felt like a Brillo Pad, and a normal chunk of love with markings similar to Iris's.

We talked to Cassi Anderson, a breeder living on nearby Whidbey Island specializing in hairless and dwarf rats, whom I knew from Facebook. She displayed a big blue ribbon she'd won for Best Kitten. The adorable kitten rat baby had lost points for "curling on edges" of the ears, a head that was "too pointy or blocky at nose," and eyes deemed by the judges "squinty/very small," but in all other areas—body, show condition, temperament, tail, eyes, and markings—she was perfect. She was not, however, for sale.

Then we talked to the organizer, a woman named Lynn who bred rats in Seattle not far from where Ellie and Jonah lived and who had designed the Ratapalooza logo to look like that of Starbucks. She had, she said, about sixty rats at home.

I said, "You don't have two extras we could take home?"

"No, they're my babies."

"Sixty of them?"

"Yes!"

She didn't have any litters now because, she explained, a virus that caused miscarriages and deformities in babies had been going around the local community and all the local breeders had stopped production. She said she would start again soon, and so in three weeks she should have babies, who would be available six or seven weeks after they were born.

"That's months from now," I said. I may have emitted a small whining or moaning noise as well.

I had counted on spending the rest of my weekend in Seattle playing with baby rats at Ellie and Jonah's house (while rodent-slaughtering Helen waited outside in the fenced-in yard).

"Oh come on," I said as Ellie and Jonah slunk away, embarrassed by my persistence. "Let us have a couple of rats."

"Well," Lynn said, "you could have Captain Chumley." And then she gave an evil snigger. "He doesn't like anyone." But I knew she was as likely to give up Captain Chumley as I was to hand over Helen to a stranger.

Ellie collected the business cards of the two breeders who lived near her and we left Ratapalooza, ratless in Seattle. We drowned our sorrows in artisanal ice cream and a two-hour walk in Discovery Park, where Ellie and I each took seven hundred Instagram photos of Helen climbing trees, chasing birds, and looking generally majestic.

On the drive back to Spokane the next day I thought about that room in the community center, about all those people who loved rats as much as I did. All the cages had signs that said "Do Not Stick Fingers in the Cages," but whenever anyone asked to hold a rat, they got a rat to hold. You couldn't generalize about the people any more than you could about the rats. Young, old, purple hair, gray hair, hipsters, codgers, we were all there, different as you could imagine and united by our devotion to these affectionate creatures generally thought unlovable.

Back at home I cuddled with my predatory canine, slayer of squirrels and marmots, chaser of cats, eavesdropper on conversations, owner of hundreds of stuffed animals, hogger of bed space, evangelist for doghood, kisser of strange men in bars.

"I love you, Helen," I said, and as she always does when I say this to her, she sighed and blinked her eyes. She opened them, I said it again, and she closed them.

"I love you, Helen."

Blink.

"I love you, Helen."

Blink.

We kept this up until her eyes stayed closed and she fell asleep.

I love that dog.

But I really missed having a rat.

Helen and Laurel: bigotry and prejudice
require ignorance to thrive

The Girlfriends

Can you fall in love again?

After we struck out at Ratapalooza. Ellie got in touch with the Seattle breeders, who kept promising a litter, but no kittens were forthcoming.

When I started seeing loads of photos of baby rats on a local Facebook rat group, I tagged Ellie and told her she might want to consider expanding her rat search and make a trip back to Spokane. Next thing I knew, Ellie had been in touch with a breeder who lived near me and she had picked out two babies. Ellie does not waste time.

We started looking at the calendar. I agreed to take delivery of the rats and would keep them for a week until Ellie and Jonah could come to claim them. I would be, in other words, the foster mother.

I met the breeder in the Safeway parking lot. She was also, I knew from Facebook, a horse person. When I asked her how many rats she had, she told me forty-five breeding females.

Forty-five?

Then she confessed, "I have snakes."

She also had guinea pigs, hamsters, and chinchillas.

In the backseat of her car was a tall cage. I'd brought a cardboard box with me because Ellie had ordered everything I'd need to be delivered to my home—cage, sleeping hut, litter, water bottle, and hammock.

When the breeder grabbed the rats she held one up. The rat had a chubby white body and a gray head marked with a white blaze that looked like New York's Chrysler Building. The breeder said, "She's the troublemaker. She managed to unlatch the cage and get into the bag of litter." I peered into the car and saw litter strewn all over the backseat. "Her sister's the quiet one. She just follows."

Ellie told me that Jonah had already named one of the girls Fern (the follower, who had a gray head with a white marking that I thought looked like a sperm, but Ellie said was actually the state of Idaho, and splotches down her back). I decided to call the troublemaker Laurel, after the

Harvard historian Laurel Thatcher Ulrich, who wrote a phrase so good it's been put on T-shirts and bumper stickers: "Well-behaved women seldom make history." Originally I wanted to call the chubby sister Roberta, which Ellie promptly vetoed. Then I suggested Lorelei, because, come on, who doesn't love *Gilmore Girls*? Ellie said no way to that.

"Fine," I said. "I'm calling her Laurel. At least for the next week."

When Ellie took possession, she could call them whatever she wanted. My godrats have remained Fern and Laurel.

I set up their cage in my guest bedroom in order to keep them safe from Helen the would-be felon, whom I locked out. I put a paper shopping bag on the bed and let Fern and Laurel run around. At first they stayed in the bag, as I knew they would. They needed a safe place. But it didn't take long before they started to wrestle and play. They took turns chasing and pinning each other and making the bag shake and rumble. Whoever won the tussle got to groom her sister. I lay on my side and peeked into the bag as they roughhoused. Helen sat outside the closed door and every few minutes tapped gently on it with her paw.

"No, varmint killer," I said. "You're not coming in."

She'd wait a few minutes and then knock again. Helen's polite, but determined.

It didn't take long for Fern and Laurel to leave the comfort of the brown paper bag and explore the pillows, behind the pillows, and me. They were small—the size of mice—and reminded me of baby Iris. They played like puppies and then slept hard.

When I put them back into their cage I held Helen by the collar and let her into the room to sniff. At first she trembled with excitement and licked her lips. This did not make me happy and I gave her a stern warning.

Helen parked herself in front of the rat cage and watched with the same rapt fascination I bring to episodes of *The Bachelor*. The rats seemed to like Helen immediately. They came right up to her and poked their noses through the bars of the cage. Helen backed away, astonished and maybe a little frightened.

After the first day, convinced Helen wasn't going to try anything funny, I let her stay in the room while the rats ran sprints on the bed. They tumbled around in the paper bag and Helen's gigantic ears twitched and flickered. Then the rats dashed toward her and she retreated. This happened over and over and over again. We all loved it.

On the second day I held Helen's muzzle tight while Fern came close and licked her on the nose. Helen looked pained, but tolerant. Then Fern reached up and nearly climbed inside one of Helen's oversized ears. She stopped near Helen's mouth and started grooming herself. Helen, confused, stood frozen. Like Iris, Fern and Laurel had to stop messing around every few minutes to groom themselves (and each other and me and eventually Helen). I loved how they would hold one of their own arms like a baby and tend maternally to every errant hair. I loved how they'd grab a back foot as if they were playing the cello.

I gave the youngsters a variety of snacks to see if they had different tastes. One would go crazy for cucumber while the other would only eat the part without the seeds. They both adored Cheez-Its (who doesn't?) and tortilla chips. In the mornings, I'd bring my bowl of cereal onto the bed and eat it while they scrambled over my legs and onto my lap. When I finished I'd dip my fingers into the remaining milk and let them lick it off.

It was easy to see differences between these sisters. Laurel was a bruiser, bigger, fatter, faster, and more aggressive than Fern. She liked to play Whack-a-Rat, where I would tap her on the nose and she'd withdraw to the paper bag and then come charging back. She liked to box with my fingers. Whenever I offered food to both of them, Laurel would elbow Fern out of the way.

I know you're not supposed to have favorites.

Fern was my favorite. Sweeter, just as curious but more tactful, she sought contact and connection. Not just with me, but with Helen.

When I felt confident that my dog would not make a snack of Ellie's rats, I let Helen lie on the bed with us as Fern and Laurel ran around. I know what you're thinking. Crazy, right? But I also know Helen. At that point, I trusted her not to do anything to the rats. She's never taken food without permission, even when it falls on the floor.

Laurel went about her business. She'd give Helen a quick sniff and move on to some project she had going behind the pillows. Fern, however, wanted to nuzzle under Helen's chest. You would not believe how carefully Helen kept track of where the rats were, how she made sure she didn't step on them or knock them over with her tail. Fern gave Helen a manicure and a pedicure. At first Helen seemed uncertain about this kind of attention, but she soon got used to it. It didn't take long before Helen was sniffing Fern's butt like a buddy.

After a while, I stopped closing the door to the guest room when I went out. I'd come home to find Helen parked in front of the rat cage. In the evenings I'd say to Helen, "Let's go see our girlfriends," and she would dash to the guest room. When I screamed out, "GIRLFRIENDS!" Fern would poke her nose between the bars and reach out with a tiny paw to pat Helen's snout.

Naturally I had to document this beautiful interspecies friendship. I posted photos on social media of the dog that all of my friends knew as a marmot slayer posing with rats crawling on her. My friends were stunned and impressed.

Ellie seemed nervous, but I sent her text after text detailing the antics of her new pets and reassuring her that Helen treated them like honored visitors. As much as I looked forward to seeing Ellie and Jonah when they came to town, I started to dread having them take away the girlfriends.

In a few short days I had grown to love my godrats. That I could have predicted.

What surprised me was how Helen had managed to fight against her nature. All it took for her to overcome the nearly irresistible internal force of instinctive predation was a little familiarity. She may still not love the idea of rats, but becoming acquainted with Fern and Laurel taught her that you can't dismiss an entire species once you get to know some of them as individuals.

This astonished me. Biology is a lot harder to tame than prejudice or bigotry, which rely on ignorance to thrive.

Maybe, if Helen could accept the girlfriends, all those

people who say they hate rats will be able, once they get to know someone like Iris, or Sarah Jane, or Fern or Laurel, to realize that these reviled rodents are not gross or dirty or horrid. They are simply misunderstood.

At least, that's my hope.

Suggestions for Further Reading

Fiction

O'Brien, Robert C. *Mrs. Frisby and the Rats of NIMH*. New York: Atheneum Books for Young Readers, 1971.

Seidler, Tor. *A Rat's Tale*. New York: Farrar, Straus and Giroux, 1986.

Rat Care and Training

Ducommun, Debbie. *The Complete Guide to Rat Training: Tricks and Games for Rat Fun and Fitness*. Neptune City, N.J.: T.F.H. Publications, 2008.

Ducommun, Debbie. *Rats: Practical, Accurate Advice from the Expert*. Irvine, Calif.: I-5 Publishing, 2011.

General Nonfiction Books about Rats

Alderton, David. *Rodents of the World*. London: Facts on File, 1996.

Barrett, S. Anthony. *The Story of Rats: Their Impact on Us, and Our Impact on Them*. Sydney: Allen & Unwin, 2001.

Burt, Jonathan. *Rat*. London: Reaktion Books Ltd., 2006.

Darwin, Charles. *The Expression of the Emotions in Man and Animals*. London: John Murray, 1872.

Hendrickson, Robert. *More Cunning Than Man: A Complete History of the Rat and Its Role in Human Civilization*. New York: Kensington Books, 1983.*

Hodgson, Barbara. *The Rat: A Perverse Miscellany*. Berkeley: Ten Speed Press, 1997.*

Lambert, Kelly. *The Lab Rat Chronicles: A Neuroscientist Reveals Life Lessons from the Planet's Most Successful Mammals*. New York: Perigree Books, 2011.

Langton, Jerry. *Rat: How the World's Most Notorious Rodent Clawed Its Way to the Top*. New York: St. Martin's Press, 2007.*

Marriott, Edward. *The Plague Race: A Tale of Fear, Science, and Heroism*. New York: Picador, 2002.*

Panksepp, Jaak. *Affective Neuroscience: The Foundations of Human and Animal Emotions*. New York: Oxford University Press, 1998.

Sullivan, Robert. *Rats: Observations on the History and Habitat of the City's Most Unwanted Inhabitants.* New York: Bloomsbury Publishing, 2004.

*Books about the, um, less savory aspects of rats

Websites

American Fancy Rat & Mouse Association, afrma.org

R.A.T.S. Rat Assistance & Teaching Society, petrats.org

Illustration Credits

Acknowledgments

Being an author requires long hours of sitting in front of your computer and staring into space. It's lonely work, wrangling all those words onto the page. But the truth is, it takes a village to write a book. One of the funnest parts is when you get to thank those who helped you along the way. You know how people on television awards shows get all teary when they accept the statuette and then list names until the music comes on to drown them out? That's what you're getting here.

I am grateful to the many serious scientists who took time away from their own work to help me with mine: Inbal Ben-Ami Bartal, Marc Bekoff, Anne Hanson, Bernd Heinrich, Alexandra Horowitz, Kelly Lambert, Joseph LeDoux, Peggy Mason, Jaak Panksepp, Chris Robison, and Robert Timm.

Also to those fearless rat promoters who patiently answered my emails and phone calls and whose books and artwork help to convince the haters of how adorable and human our rodent friends are: Debbie Ducommun, Jessica Florence, Abby Roeser, Tor Seidler, and Ellen Van Deelen.

On Facebook I found a nest of rat-loving friends who shared personal stories and important information with me: Aria of AG Rattery, Cassi Anderson, Dee Bolen, Jen Brock, Mary Giles, Kara Loyd, the late Robin MacDonald, and Mariska Williams.

When I was ratless in Spokane, friends came to the rescue by letting me get a fix, allowing me to hold and play with their vermin. I'm still a little embarrassed that I told Sarah Jane I loved her after knowing her for only a few minutes, but that rat, belonging to Dorian Karahalios and Mariah Martin, reminded me so much of Iris I couldn't help myself. Also thanks to fellow rat mamas Tori Bumbeck, Anastasia Hilton, and Marilyn Neilson.

I'm slobberingly grateful to Iris's sitters and the FOIs (Friends of Iris): former students Ivory Coghlan, Megan Cuilla, and especially Ellie and Jonah Kozlowski, who loved Iris enough to want to get rats of their own, and then allowed me to be Auntie Rachel to Fern and Laurel. Jason Lathrop photographed my darling beautifully—and came to see that she was in fact cute. Greg Gordon allowed Iris to crawl all over him and sent interesting rat clippings my way; Chris Valeo appreciated and occasionally cared for Iris; and Natalie Kusz always invited her over for dinner. Janet and Dan Henderson fed us often and Dan answered all my medical questions, even though he's a dermatologist and can't be expected to know most of the stuff I ask him about.

Ruth Monnig is my smartest reader and the librarian of my heart. Sage, David, and Becky Brooks took both Iris and me into their lives and home. Candace Karu considered Iris her godrat. Valerie Chang has been my go-to girl for more than three and a half decades. I'm so gratified she has a daughter, Ivy, who loves animals and knows how to care for rats. Andrew Krystal is a terrible driver and a wonderful rat-loving man. When I first met Mike Bergmann all those years ago he thought dogs should live outside. He ended up loving Iris, even though I had to keep yelling at him to watch his big feet when he was in the house. Without him, I'd be lost.

I'm so fortunate to teach at Eastern Washington University, where I have great colleagues and wonderful students, some of whom are fellow rat fans. I'm particularly grateful to the EWU Research and Scholarship Committee that awarded me two summer grants so I could figure out what this book should be and eventually write it.

My agent, Elise Capron at the Sandy Dijkstra Literary Agency, has become, in the time I've known her, a doting dog mama. I am grateful for her help and support.

Often when authors get together they complain about their publishers. A lot. When I get into conversations like that, I have to leave the room. I've got nothing to contribute and people hate you when you say that you couldn't be happier with how you've been treated. The folks at Farrar Straus Giroux Books for Young Readers and Macmillan Kids are, simply, the best in the business. While I'm a little disappointed that editorial director Joy Peskin decided to get a guinea pig instead of a rat, the photos of Ginger on Facebook make me think I've underestimated the pigs. I'm thrilled to be a far-flung member of the MacRunners and proudly wear a team singlet, designed by Andrew Arnold, who also designed this book. Molly Brouillette has been a dream publicist, especially for an author who hates doing publicity. And while I've long sung the praises of copy editors, Karla Reganold and her team deserve candy, flowers, a pony, and a parade for catching so many of my childish mistakes. About my editor, Wes Adams, I have nothing to say. Except that he changed my life, and for him I would run a marathon over hot coals while juggling pumpkins and playing the piano.